A GRIM ALMANAC OF

EDINBURGH & THE LOTHIANS

Edinburgh Castle from the Vennel, early 1900s. (Author's Collection)

A GRIM ALMANAC OF

EDINBURGH & THE LOTHIANS

ALAN SHARP

The History Press

Captain Henderson, Chief Constable of Edinburgh. (S.P. Evans)

First published 2009

The History Press
The Mill, Brimscombe Port
Stroud, Gloucestershire, GL5 2QG
www.thehistorypress.co.uk

British Library Cataloguing in Publication Data.
A catalogue record for this book is available from the British Library.

ISBN 978 0 7509 5105 0

Typesetting and origination by The History Press
Printed in Great Britain

CONTENTS

ACKNOWLEDGEMENTS

A book of this nature is never a solo achievement. To the many people and institutions who have helped me along the way I would like to say a warm thank you.

I would first particularly like to thank the staff of the Edinburgh Room of the Central Library – where I spent long hours finding many of the stories that appear in this book – who were never less than courteous and always ready to give their help in any way possible.

I would also like to thank the staff of the following institutions who have helped me along the way: the National Library of Scotland, the National Museum of Scotland, the Edinburgh City Chambers, and the Real Mary King's Close Visitor Attraction.

There are a number of individuals who have helped me with my facts, pointed me in the direction of interesting stories, or helped me to gather together the illustrations for this volume. In no particular order I would like to thank: Stewart P. Evans, Richard Whittington-Egan, Adrian Smith, Stuart Hamilton, Lesley Gracie, Peter Stubbs, Kay Bohan, and the staff of Edinburgh Books.

Finally I would like to thank the three women in my life for their love and support during the writing of this book: my mother Rose, my daughter Hannah, and my beautiful partner Estella. I don't know how they put up with me!

INTRODUCTION

From the very earliest days, man has always been fascinated with the dark side of life. Death, violence, war and the supernatural, these are elements of tales going right back to the days of Homer, and most likely centuries earlier. It satisfies some primal need within us.

In the days of the Roman Empire we visited the amphitheatres to see criminals thrown to wild animals or hacked to pieces by gladiators. In the Middle Ages it was public executions. And as life became more civilized, more sedate, as these real life horrors became no longer available to us, we turned to literature, theatre and later film and television to get our bloodthirsty daily fix. It is no coincidence that the rise of the Victorian gothic novel coincided with the change in the law which hid hangings from the public view.

If there is one city on earth indelibly associated with horror, it is Edinburgh. The haunted city, its reputation for ghosts and ghouls, witchcraft and murderous dealings in the darkened wynds and closes, is second to none. The city today thrives on it, with countless ghostly graveyard tours leaving from the Mercat Cross, former site of public executions, or from the front of St Giles' Cathedral – where the gloomy Tollbooth Gaol once stood – every night of the year come rain or shine.

Edinburgh is a city steeped in history. It is like two cities in one. The Georgian splendour of the New Town, and the grid-like structure of the Victorian tenements to the south of the Meadows hide within them the medieval Old Town, where the gentility of those surrounding districts falls away and one can almost feel gripped by the city's grim and violent past.

The New Town is a city of culture and education. Through its streets walked many of the most brilliant minds of their day, from literary giants like Sir Walter Scott, Robert Louis Stephenson and Arthur Conan Doyle, to the great artists and thinkers, Adam Smith, David Hume, Charles Darwin, Sir Henry Raeburn, Alexander Graham Bell and James Boswell.

But there in the Old Town, in the grimy plague-ridden streets, the characters that haunt our nightmares walked. Major Weir, the devil-worshipping wizard and his wicked sister Grizel; Captain Porteous, the corrupt and murderous official who inspired the city to mob justice; Deacon Brodie, respectable gent by day, criminal fiend by night. And worst of all, Burke and Hare, the grave robbers whose greed led them to speed up their trade by no longer waiting for the merchandise to die.

All of these stories and many more can be found within these pages. In a city like Edinburgh they are not hard to find. Tales of murder and arson, pestilence and plague, running battles through the streets, political schemes and underhanded dirty deeds. Through all the echelons of society, from the itinerants and beggars who struggled to find a crust to eat in the filth-ridden tenements, through scheming, back-stabbing city officials, to noblemen and even Kings and Queens, their evil crimes are recorded here for all time.

A tomb in Greyfriar's Kirkyard featuring macabre carvings. (Author's Collection)

So let me take you by the hand, and together we will wander through the pages of history. Together we will bear witness to the foul deeds which await us around every corner. By my side you will see the monsters and fiends which lurk in the shadows and haunt our nightmares. Come on, you're safe with me; I know the way. But be careful not to stray from the path. You never know what might be waiting to jump out . . .

JANUARY

EUGÈNE MARIE CHANTRELLE, now or lately prisoner in the prison of Edinburgh, you are Indicted and Accused at the instance of the Right Honourable WILLIAM WATSON, Her Majesty's Advocate for Her Majesty's interest: THAT ALBEIT, by the laws of this and of every other well-governed realm, MURDER is a crime of an heinous nature, and severely punishable: YET TRUE IT IS AND OF VERITY, that you the said Eugène Marie Chantrelle are guilty of the said crime, actor, or art and part: IN SO FAR AS, on the

1st or 2d day of January 1878,

Tuesday or Wednesday

or on one or other of the days of December immediately preceding, within the dwelling-house in or near George Street, Edinburgh, then occupied by you the said Eugène Marie Chantrelle, you did, wickedly and feloniously, administer to, or cause to be taken by, Elizabeth Cullen Dyer or Chantrelle, your wife, now deceased, then residing with you, in an orange or part or parts thereof, and in lemonade, or in one or other of those articles, or in some other article of food or drink to the prosecutor unknown, or in some other manner to the prosecutor unknown, a quantity or quantities of opium or other poison to the prosecutor unknown; and the said Elizabeth Cullen Dyer or Chantrelle having taken the said opium or other poison by you administered or caused to be taken as aforesaid, did, in consequence thereof, die on the said 2d day of January 1878, and was thus murdered by you the said Eugène Marie Chantrelle: And you the said Eugène Marie Chantrelle had previously evinced malice and ill-will towards the said Elizabeth Cullen Dyer or Chantrelle, and, on many occasions between the time of your marriage with her in the month of August 1868 and the date of her death aforesaid, had falsely accused her to other persons of adultery and of incest, and struck and otherwise maltreated and abused her, and threatened to shoot her and to poison her, and by your violence and your threatenings put her in fear of losing her life: And you the said Eugène Marie Chantrelle having been apprehended and taken before Thomas Rowatt, Esquire, one of the magistrates of the city of Edinburgh, did, in his presence at Edinburgh, on each of the

8th and 9th days of January 1878,

Official indictment of Eugène Chantrelle. (S.P. Evans)

1 JANUARY 1573

Life in Edinburgh in the Middle Ages was always likely to be disturbed by occasional outbreaks of violence. At this time the whole country was in a precarious state. The monarch, Mary Queen of Scots, was in exile after the murder of her husband, and control rested with the Regent Morton, the whole country having capitulated except Edinburgh Castle, which lay under the control of Sir William Kirkaldy, a man fiercely loyal to his queen. Morton had been attempting to wrest the castle from Kirkaldy for fully three years, and on the date in question a truce between the two expired. At six o'clock that morning Kirkaldy, aware that the city was occupied by many English troops brought in by Morton, had a warning gun fired, announcing that all those loyal to the Queen should retire. Whereupon he opened fire with the cannons of the castle, firing cannonballs indiscriminately into the city streets. There were heavy casualties, especially in the fish market where many of the shots fell, and under cover of the cannonade Kirkaldy rode out of the castle and set fire to the houses in the West Bow and Castle Wynd. Kirkaldy finally surrendered the castle in May of that year, after several weeks of bombardment from five batteries of guns, and was hanged on 3 August.

Edinburgh Castle as it looked before the siege of 1573. (Author's Collection)

2 JANUARY 1878

On the morning of this day, servant Mary Byrne entered the bedchamber of Elizabeth Chantrelle in her George Street home to find her mistress unconscious and her bed and person covered in vomit. Calling immediately for the woman's husband, Frenchman Eugène, she left to attend to the couple's children while the man attempted to rouse his wife. On her return, Eugène commented on the smell of gas, and although Mary had not noticed this earlier, it was now quite marked. The family doctor, on arriving, also noticed a strong smell of gas, the supply of which had, by now, been cut off at the meter. As such, gas poisoning was suspected as the cause when the patient died that afternoon without regaining consciousness. However, a post-mortem examination quickly showed this not to be the case, and while no sign of poison was found in the body, an examination of the vomit on the bedclothes found traces of opium. Eugène Chantrelle quickly fell under suspicion. A teacher of French, he had in fact studied as a medical practitioner and had boasted previously of his knowledge of untraceable poisons. His wife had been a pupil who had fallen pregnant by him at the age of 15, objected to what she felt was a forced marriage, and often complained of ill-treatment at his hands in their ten years together, including frequent beatings and open infidelities. He had taken out an insurance policy on her accidental death less than a year before, worth £1,000. The evidence against him, though circumstantial, was strong, and included the fact that the leak in the gas pipe in her room was shown to have been deliberately caused, and that Mary Byrne testified that she smelled no gas when she had first entered the room. Eugène Chantrelle was found guilty and sentenced to be hanged. He went to his death continuing to protest his innocence.

At his trial, medical evidence was given by Dr Joseph Bell, whose methodical detective work in laying the trail of guilt to Eugène's door would inspire his assistant, Arthur Conan Doyle, to create the character of Sherlock Holmes.

Top-floor apartments at 81A George Street, the home of Eugène and Elizabeth Chantrelle and the scene of her murder. (Author's Collection)

Dr Joseph Bell, forensic examiner on the Chantrelle case, and mentor to Arthur Conan Doyle. (Mary Evans Picture Library)

3 JANUARY 1929

Seven-year-old David Mack and his friend Gordon Strachan were skating this day on a frozen stretch of the Union Canal near Viewforth Bridge when the surface gave way, plunging both boys into the icy-cold water. When the two were eventually fished out, Mack was dead and Strachan, suffering from severe shock, was admitted to the Royal Infirmary.

4 JANUARY 1732

At eight o'clock on this morning, in the home of Widow Welsh, a butter-maker, at the head of the West Bow, a maidservant raking the fire in the good Widow's bedroom, where she lay sick, accidentally set fire to a large quantity of butter which sat nearby. Flames from the oily butter soon reached a great height, catching the whole room alight. Mistress and maid narrowly managed to escape with their lives, and the fire engine was called. Being at a great height in the building, the water from the engine was unable to reach the room and the firemen were reduced to carrying water up ladders in buckets. One of the ladders broke under the weight of the men, causing several serious injuries, but the fire was eventually extinguished without spreading to other apartments. However, Widow Welsh, from the strain of what had happened, fell down dead shortly afterwards.

5 JANUARY 1886

A ridiculous row over a donkey's ears led to a fatal altercation on this date. Thomas Scott and Thomas Adamson were proceeding along Spring Gardens in Abbeyhill in a cart pulled by the donkey in question when three men who were clearly the worse for drink approached them. The men began to make fun of the donkey and one, Alexander Cunningham, proposed cutting off its ears. Scott, at this point, leapt from the cart and began to argue with the men, the argument leading to blows being struck with one James Allan. The men departed at this point, but the two parties met again near Holyrood Palace and the quarrel was renewed. During this second altercation Scott was knocked down by the third man, James Graham, and, on getting to his feet, drew a knife and stabbed him in the chest. A doctor was quickly summoned who recommended sending Graham to the infirmary, but he died before he could be conveyed there.

6 JANUARY 1830

William Adams, a 20-year-old from a respectable Edinburgh family, was executed on this day for robbery. His crime was that he had followed a man named Michael Pirnie, a mason, from the Cowgate, through a narrow dark passage which led to the Backstairs and from there to the High Street. As they approached the foot of the stairs, Adams struck Pirnie a blow to the head from behind with his fist, and when the man fell to the ground began to punch and kick him until he was insensible. He then relieved the man's pockets of a £1 note, 4s and 8d in coins and a tin snuff box before making his escape.

7 JANUARY 1863

Alexander Milne, an Irish immigrant who ran a jeweller's shop in Frederick Street, had been made bankrupt in 1860, after which he took to drink and the balance of his mind appeared to his friends somewhat altered. He often sent work to James Paterson, a working jeweller of St James' Square, and the pair had become friendly and visited one another regularly. However, around Christmas time of 1862, Milne took it into his head that Paterson, an unmarried man, was trying to poison him and his children and had designs upon his wife. On 6 January 1863, Milne ordered a pair of Albert mounts from Paterson. Paterson believed that he was the worse for drink or fever at the time, and the following morning sent one of his men round to make a guarded inquiry as to whether he remembered ordering them. Milne replied that he did, and asked that Paterson himself should come to see him, which he did later that morning. No sooner had he entered the shop than Milne accused him of trying to make away with his wife, and when Paterson laughed at the suggestion Milne stabbed him in the chest with a knife he had purchased a day or two earlier. Paterson managed to stagger out of the shop and onto the street from where he was helped to a nearby baker's shop, and assistance was sent for. But by the time a doctor arrived from a nearby pharmacy there was little to be done, and Paterson died within five minutes of his arrival.

8 JANUARY 1752

The murder of a master or mistress by a servant was looked on as a very serious affair indeed in eighteenth-century Scotland, and one to be punished with the strictest severity so that noble folk could feel safe in their own houses. One of the most celebrated cases was the murder of Lady Baillie by footman Norman Ross. Ross, a young man from Inverness, had travelled over much of Europe as valet to a military officer before finding himself in the service of Mrs Hume, the sister of the Laird of Baillie, who divided her time between homes in Edinburgh and Berwick-upon-Tweed. Having fallen into intemperate habits, Ross occupied his off-duty hours drinking, gambling and fornicating with the livery servants, one of whom he was unfortunate to get into the family way and found himself having to supply money to both her and his illegitimate child. At first he attempted to find the money by borrowing from fellow servants and acquaintances, but soon it became obvious that he would need to find another source, and at length settled on the idea of robbing his mistress. Breaking into her upstairs bedroom at Brunstane House, while Lady Baillie was asleep, he began to search the room for money or jewellery, when the noise of opening a desk drawer accidentally woke her by. Realising he was about to be detected, he swiftly seized a knife which lay on the desk and slit her throat. In panic he then leapt from the bedroom window intending to make good his escape, but broke his leg in the fall and was only able to crawl away to secrete himself in a nearby cornfield. On the discovery of the body the following morning by the woman's two daughters, a search of the property discovered a hat belonging to Ross below the window, and his shoes at the bedroom door. An investigation of the surroundings was quickly instituted which turned up the criminal within the day, and Ross was taken away to stand trial. His sentence was to be hanged at the Gallow Lee, but first to have his right hand struck off and affixed to the top of the gibbet with the murder weapon. His body was hung in chains to rot.

9 JANUARY 1822

There may be some glamour associated with pirates in our modern day, but in truth piracy was anything but a glamorous business. On this day Peter Heaman and Francois Gautiez were hanged for piracy and murder on a gallows erected on the sands of Leith at the high water mark. Gautiez had been the cook and Heaman the mate aboard the schooner *Jane*, bound from Gibraltar to Brazil and carrying a large sum of money, amounting to $38,180 Spanish dollars. Tempted by the money, the pair killed the captain, Thomas Johnston, and another seaman, James Paterson, and forced the rest of the crew into aiding them while they sailed the schooner to the isle of Lewis, where they put ashore with the money and sunk the

Brunstane House. (Author's Collection)

vessel. The pair were quickly arrested on the information of a Maltese cabin boy, Andrew Camelier, and transported to the naval yard at Leith where they were tried before the High Court of the Admiralty, under whose jurisdiction all crimes at sea lay. Initially, they fabricated a story whereby the captain had killed Paterson before the rest of the crew turned on him, and that the crew had decided by mutual consent to secrete the money. After conviction they confessed their crimes and were given an opportunity to make their peace before being dispatched to eternity.

10 JANUARY 1743

The *Edinburgh Courant* recorded on this date the death in captivity of an 80-year-old prisoner named Mackintosh of Borlum, who had been held in Edinburgh Castle since being part of a Jacobite attempt to storm the castle in 1715. It had been thwarted after one of the participants' wives had warned the authorities.

11 JANUARY 1832

A man by the name of Robertson was brought before the Police Court accused of inhumanly beating his wife and father-in-law, a man of 82 years of age. Witnesses, including the man's stepson, testified to Robertson having made a regular habit of mistreating his wife, and on this occasion he was said to have knocked one of the old man's teeth out. The elderly victim stated that he was lucky to be alive, and that had it not been for the protection of the police he would have surely been murdered. The Baillie, expressing his abhorrence of the crime, sentenced the man to sixty days hard labour in the Bridewell Prison.

12 JANUARY 1708

Robert Baird and Robert Oswald were enjoying a night out in Leith when Baird decided that a drinking contest should ensue. Oswald was less keen on the idea and began to refuse drinks, to which Baird took offence, demanding an apology from him for poor manners. Oswald refused and the evening went on in bad humour until eventually the two gentlemen left and took a coach back to Edinburgh. Alighting by the Netherbow, Baird drew his sword and ran his friend through twice, inflicting a mortal wound. He was later pardoned on the grounds that the act was not a 'forethought felony'.

13 JANUARY 1590

Here is an interesting example of the judicial system in action in medieval Scotland. On this day King James VI was presiding over the courts in Edinburgh and hearing the case of the Laird of Craigmillar, who was suing his wife for divorce, when the Earl of Bothwell burst into the proceedings and forcibly removed one of the witnesses, took him away to his castle eleven miles distant and informed him that if he uttered a word in evidence in the court he would hang him like a dog.

14 JANUARY 1720

A fast was held on this day in Calder, West Lothian, for the son of Lord Torpichen, who had become known as the 'devil boy'. The Hon. Patrick Sandilands, as his title ran, had become erratic in his behaviour to the point that most in the district considered him bewitched or possessed of an evil spirit. It was said that he often fell down in trances, or would be thrown about a room as if some unseen agent were controlling him. He could tell people of things that were happening out of his sight or a long distance away, and claimed to be able to travel long distances out of his own body. Candles were said to go out in his presence. The blame was placed on a woman in the village who had long been suspected of witchcraft, and under torture she confessed and implicated two others. However, the practice of burning witches having by this time ceased, the supposed culprits were merely imprisoned.

15 JANUARY 1920

Nobody ever knew what it was that former soldier Neil Quinn and his wife Elizabeth had their last argument about. It was only when a neighbour heard a disturbance at her door and opened it to find the pair dying at her feet that anyone realised something desperate had happened. The pair had been well liked in the district, and an hour earlier Quinn had been seen returning home with some onions, which were found cooking on the stove of the apartment along with some sausages. As far as could be discerned, Quinn had cut his wife's throat with a razor before using the weapon on himself in the same way. When his wife had escaped his grasp and run through the front door he followed, but neither managed to get more than a few feet before becoming too weak from blood loss to continue any further.

16 JANUARY 1682

A prime example of the old idiom 'he who lives by the sword ...' One Alexander Cockburn was this day condemned to be hanged for the murder of a man named Adamson, a blue-gown or licensed beggar so known because of the blue gowns they wore to indicate their legal status. In fact the evidence against Cockburn was purely circumstantial – no body having been produced – but the sounds of murder had been heard coming from his house and bloody clothes found therein. The irony is that Cockburn, at this time, was the official hangman for Edinburgh.

17 JANUARY 1746

Fleeing from defeat at the Battle of Falkirk, which occurred on this date, Lieutenant General Henry Hawley and his troops stopped at the Palace of Linlithgow in West Lothian where he demanded the best of victuals for his men from the housekeeper, Mrs Glen Gordon. Following the meal, against the strong remonstrances of their host, they showed their gratitude by setting the palace on fire and burning it to a shell before departing.

18 JANUARY 1925

While walking in the Royal Botanic Garden on this date, one young sightseer's curiosity was aroused by a lady's coat and hat lying at the foot of a yew tree near the glass houses. On closer inspection he found the lady herself hanging from the branches of the tree some 15ft above the ground. Olive Green, a 34-year-old medical student and widow of a chaplain who had been killed during the First World War, had apparently taken her own life due to nervous exhaustion, using her own scarf to carry out the deed.

The Royal Botanic Garden. (Author's Collection)

19 JANUARY 1595

The conclusion to a dispute which had raged for over two years came this day. The argument had begun in a legal litigation over some land for which a deed had been forged. The losing litigant, Sir James Sandilands, had become enraged at his opponent, John Graham, a judge at the Court of Session. Graham, having been advised to quit Edinburgh in the interests of the peace, had been doing so on 19 February 1593, when he was set upon and killed by Sandilands and a party of supporters in Leith Wynd. The Earl of Montrose, as head of the Family of Graham, took it on himself to avenge his clansman's death, and made it known that he was coming to Edinburgh to do just that. Sandilands, hoping to gain the upper hand, resolved to attack the Earl's party as soon as it arrived. A running battle in the High Street was soon so fierce that the magistrates and other inhabitants of the town barricaded themselves in their houses with weapons for their own protection. Eventually the fight was broken up, by which time Sandilands lay shot and stabbed several times through the body and survived only through the skilled work of a surgeon by the name of Captain Lockheart. Several others on his side, and one man on Montrose's, were not so lucky.

20 JANUARY 1564

Protestant reformer John Knox wrote: 'God from heaven, and upon the face of the earth, gave declaration that he was offended at the iniquity that was committed within this realm; for, upon the 20th day of January, there fell weet [water] in great abundance, whilk [which] in the falling freezit so vehemently, that the earth was but ane sheet of ice. The fowls both great and small freezit, and micht not flie: mony died, and some were taken and laid beside the fire, that their feathers might resolve. And in that same month, the sea stood still, as was clearly observed, and neither ebbed nor flowed the space of twenty-four hours.'

John Knox. (Author's Collection)

21 JANUARY 1904

Robert Robertson, a commercial traveller from Dysart, was somewhat the worse for drink after a long lunch when he hired the cab driven by Robert Cadden at Waterloo Place. Agreeing to pay the man 2s per hour for three hours of work, he was taken around the city to various stops where he called on customers who owed him money. However, after around an hour and a half of driving, during which Robertson became progressively more intoxicated, Cadden took it into his head to relieve him of the money accrued so far. Calling on another cabbie, Robert Dodds, to drive his cab, Cadden went inside with the man and beat and half strangled him while rifling his pockets for the money. Cadden and Dodds then attempted to drive away, whereupon Robertson got in front of the horses to prevent them. Dodds struck the man with the whip, causing him to fall unconscious tn the ground, and the cab then drove away, running over his legs in the process. The two men were each sentenced to forty days hard labour.

22 JANUARY 1911

While walking in the Hermitage Park on the Braid Hills just outside Edinburgh, Eric Wilson discovered the body of a young woman lying in the grass. She had been strangled, and had been lying there some six hours according to the doctor's estimate. PC George Irvine, who had been patrolling near the spot throughout the night, reported having seen and heard nothing to attract his attention. The unfortunate woman was Maria Jane Boyle, a married woman and mother of two children. Her husband reported that she had, of late, contracted intemperate habits, and that she had gone out around 7.30 p.m. on the previous night saying she was going to her mother's, and had not returned. Her mother had not seen her that day. A man named Alexander Wyse was initially arrested because he had been seen that morning with blood on him and had been acting suspiciously. No evidence was found to connect him with the deceased woman, and no subsequent arrest was ever made.

23 JANUARY 1570

When James Stuart, 1st Earl of Moray, was murdered on this day in Linlithgow, he made history as the first public figure to be assassinated with a firearm. Moray, acting as Regent at the time for James VI, was shot by James Hamilton of Bothwell-Haugh, a supporter of Mary Queen of Scots, whose abdication in favour of her son had been forced, and whose attempt to return to power had been thwarted by Moray at the Battle of Langside. Hamilton fired the fatal shot from the window of a house, then made his escape on a horse which he had previously tied up at the rear.

24 JANUARY 1934

In a curious echo of the Maria Boyle case (see 22 January), on this date the body of another young woman strangled in a park in the hills around Edinburgh was found by police. A man named Alexander Toomey was arrested for the crime. In this case the scene was Hunter's Bog on the lower slopes of Arthur's Seat, and the victim was 21-year-old Margaret (or Rita) McMillan. She had been seen several times the previous night in the company of a young man, and her body was discovered after the police were informed that an attack had taken place on the hillside. Toomey, a 26-year-old Leith man, was arrested after relatives informed police of his strange behaviour on the morning of the murder, and was later identified as the man with whom McMillan had been seen. When found, Margaret's body was said to be in

James Stuart, 1st Earl of Moray. (Author's Collection)

a state of near undress, and she had been strangled with a necktie and a portion of her own clothing. At trial Toomey pleaded not guilty to murder, but guilty to culpable homicide on the grounds that he had been in a state of mental weakness at the time of the murder. He was sent to prison for fifteen years.

25 JANUARY 1815

Only vague details of this story still exist. A pair of Irish criminals by the names of Kelly and O'Neill had been convicted of a crime in the countryside but escaped, fleeing to Edinburgh.

Being apprehended and placed in the Tollbooth Gaol, they could not be held there because they had been convicted of no crime within the city. Their crimes being considered quite brutal, the populace did not want to see them escape justice. As such, the High Constable of the city conducted them, at the head of a large throng, to the very limits of his jurisdiction on the Morningside road, where the party was met by the Sheriff Clerk of the county, who had them strung up from a nearby thorn tree. Their bodies were then buried by the side of the road.

26 JANUARY 1681

Little illustrates the problems of a society where the strictures of the Church become points of law like the case of four women hanged this day in Edinburgh, each on a charge of murdering their own child born out of wedlock. This was a common crime, performed in order to avoid the ignominy of being pilloried by the Church as a sinner against God, which an unmarried mother might be expected to endure. Although the Duke of York, later King James VII, took an especial interest in the matter and suggested that such women might be better dealt with through civil punishment, the Church continued to reserve the right to force them into public penitence.

27 JANUARY 1896

Mrs Cowen Guthrie, wife of a well-known doctor from the Trinity hospital, was walking towards Edinburgh by the Warriston road when she was assaulted by James Downie, a 35-year-old bootmaker who had been released from a mental establishment the previous year, where he had been incarcerated for violent behaviour. Two gravediggers in nearby Warriston cemetery witnessed the attack and quickly rushed to the lady's assistance, whereupon her assailant ran in the direction of Canonmills and was apprehended by a coachman. Another bystander made to help Mrs Guthrie, when he found a pocketknife lodged in her back between her shoulders. It was later discovered she had been stabbed a total of five times, four in the back and once in the left arm.

28 JANUARY 1829: The West Port Murders

Of all the tales of murder within the city of Edinburgh, none is so well known as that of Mr William Burke and Mr William Hare, the infamous West Port murderers whose official tally of sixteen victims makes them one of the most prolific killing teams in history. What many do not realise, however, is that only one of the pair found justice, Hare having been offered immunity from prosecution in return for testifying against his former partner. Burke was executed by hanging on this date on a scaffold erected in the High Street at the head of Libberton Wynd. The largest crowd ever assembled for a public execution gathered, some 25,000-strong, while the occupants of houses surrounding the site made large sums of money selling places at their windows for several shillings or even as much as £1 for the best views. Other hardy souls clambered onto rooftops to obtain the best possible viewpoint. Among the crowd that day was the famed Scottish author Sir Walter Scott, who ensured a prime position be reserved for him. Burke was led to the scaffold at around eight o'clock, and by ten past he was dangling by his neck from the rope.

29 JANUARY 1829: The West Port Murders

Justice having caught up with at least one of the notorious pair, William Burke was, on the day following his execution, subjected to one final indignity which might be termed poetic justice.

EXECUTION of WILLIAM BURKE.

taken on the spot.

Published by Thomas Ireland Jun.ʳ Edinburgh.

The execution of William Burke. (Mary Evans Picture Library)

The sentence of the court was that he not only be hanged, but that after death his body be publicly dissected for the purposes of anatomical education by the famed Dr Monro. On the day, crowds gathered around Surgeon's Square hoping to be admitted to the lecture, during which Monro was due to dissect the brain of the famous killer. When the size of the venue did not admit entry, rioting broke out, and to quell the crowd it was announced that Burke's body would be put on display the following day to all who wished to view it. Monro then went ahead with the dissection, which involved sawing off the cap of the skull and removing the brain. During the viewing on the 30th, it was said that 25,000 people, the same number that had attended the execution, queued patiently and filed past the corpse, which then showed the marks of the previous day's work, the skull having been crudely sewn back together.

30 JANUARY 1603

The corpse of Francis Mowbray was found on this day at the foot of Castle Rock with his neck broken. Mowbray, a Catholic who had involved himself in the same treasonous groups as would later attempt the gunpowder plot against Parliament, had been denounced by an Italian fencer named Daniel, and the matter was to be settled by a single combat between the pair in the great close at Holyrood House. However, before the appointed day, word was received from London that witnesses had been found to prove his disloyalty to the Crown. When the witnesses were brought forward they were found deficient, and Mowbray, speaking on his own account of his devotion to the King, stated, 'If ever I thought evil, or intended evil against my prince, God, that marketh the secrets of all hearts, make me fall at my enemies' feet – make me a spectacle to all Edinburgh, and cast my soul in hell forever!' Apparently God was listening, for according to the official report, Mowbray had attempted to escape confinement in the castle by sewing his bed sheets together and letting himself over the wall, but the line being too short he fell some 200ft to his death. The escape attempt being taken as a tacit admission of guilt, his lifeless corpse was dragged backwards through the streets on a hurdle to the Courts of Judiciary, where he was found guilty of his crime and posthumously hung, drawn and quartered.

31 JANUARY 1694

Carrying on an adulterous affair behind his wife's back, writer Daniel Nicolson and his widowed lover, a woman by the name of Pringle, embarked upon a scheme whereby they would frame the poor woman and her sister for an attempt on his life in order that they could be free to marry. As such, they forged a receipt in her name for a quantity of poison. The facts presented before a jury, they were found guilty both of the adultery and the forgery, the two verdicts being adjudged to have aggravated each other enough for a death sentence to be appropriate; Nicolson by hanging and Pringle by beheading.

FEBRUARY

*Henry Stuart, Lord Darnley, husband
of Mary Queen of Scots.
(Author's Collection)*

1 FEBRUARY 1728

One of Edinburgh's best-known stories is that of Maggie Dickson, or 'Half Hangit Maggie', after whom a public house in the Grassmarket is today named. A resident of Mussleburgh, where she brought up her children alone after her husband had been press-ganged into the Navy, she had an affair with a local man which resulted in her falling pregnant. Fearing the ignominy of having a child out of wedlock, she decided to keep the matter a secret. When the child either died at birth or was stillborn, she was found guilty under the Act of 1690 of concealing a pregnancy, and was sentenced to death by hanging. On this date she was taken to the Grassmarket, where the sentence was carried out in the usual manner. The execution concluded with the customary pulling down on the legs by the hangman in order to ensure that death would be swift. Maggie's body was straight away taken down from the gallows, placed in her coffin, and the lid nailed shut. The coffin was then loaded onto a cart by her family and conveyed away towards her birthplace, where she had requested to be buried. As it was usual practice for the bodies of hanged felons to be made available to medical students for dissection, a squabble broke out between the family and some surgeons who wished to take the corpse for that purpose. During the altercation the lid of the coffin was damaged, allowing air to circulate within. About two miles further on the family stopped for refreshments, and while the cart sat at the side of the road, a pair of joiners hurrying to a job heard noises coming from within the coffin. Quickly removing the lid, they were surprised when the deceased sat bolt upright, apparently much revived from her ordeal! Although somewhat confused and delirious for a few days afterwards, Maggie eventually made a full recovery, complaining only of a sore neck. Furthermore, she was now able to avail herself of a strange anomaly of Scottish law that said that, her sentence having been carried out, she had been fully punished for her crime and was now at liberty to continue her life, albeit being

A large crowd gathers for an execution in the Grassmarket. (Author's Collection)

legally dead. Although there is no record of the exact date of her eventual death, it is known that Maggie was still alive in 1753 and was a familiar figure in the city.

2 FEBRUARY 1779

Sectarian violence in Scotland is very much in the news these days, but today's troubles are as nothing compared with earlier centuries. In 1778 the English Parliament lifted the penal laws which prevented Catholics from owning property and made a significant step towards Catholic emancipation. Attempts to further loosen the laws enraged the population of Edinburgh, and on this date a mob was raised up, including some 500 sailors from Leith, who rampaged through the streets with cries of 'No Popery', breaking open the houses of known Catholics and beating them. The Catholic chapel in Chambers Close was burned to the ground and others were ransacked and plundered.

3 FEBRUARY 1700

A fire that broke out in a corner of the Fish Market at 10 p.m. on the night of 2 February quickly got out of hand, and by the following morning half the city was in flames in what was one of the worst disasters in Edinburgh's history. In a letter to his brother written on the 6th, Duncan Forbes described the damage: 'There are burned, by the easiest computation, betwixt three and four hundred families; all the pride of Edinburgh is sunk; from the Cowgate to the High Street all is burned, and hardly one stone left upon another.' He continues, 'Few people are lost, if any at all, but there was neither heart nor hand left among them for saving from

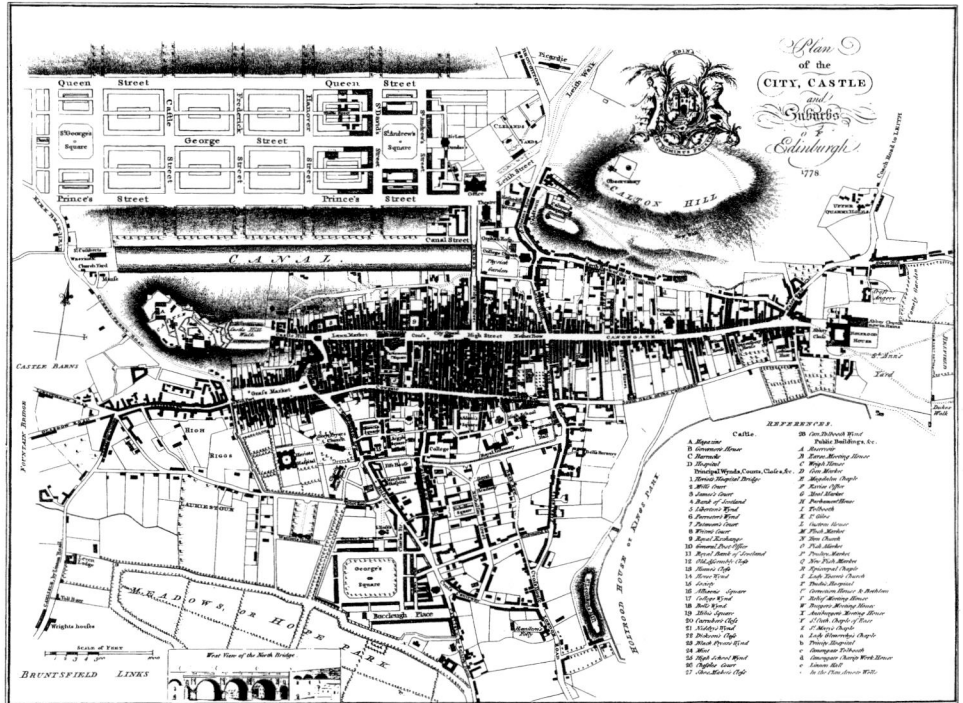

Map of Edinburgh, 1778. (Author's Collection)

the fire, nor a drop of water in the cisterns; twenty thousand hands flitting their trash, and hardly 20 at work. These babells, of ten and fourteen storeys high, are down to the ground, and their fall is very terrible ... The Fish Market, and all from the Cowgate to Pett's Street Close burned; the Exchange, vaults and coal cellars under Parliament Close are still burning. This epitome of dissolution I send you without saying any more, but that the Lord is angry with us and I see no intercessor.'

4 FEBRUARY 1881

A series of outrages occurred across the city on this night, all perpetrated by two men recently arrived from Australia, one of whom, on capture, took his own life rather than submit to arrest. They began by attacking a Mr Robert Veitch, a commercial traveller, on the Queensferry road at around 6 p.m. Vietch managed to escape his assailants by striking one on the head with an umbrella, and ran to his father's home nearby. His father and sister then joined him to search for the assailants and, on discovering them, were fired upon with pistols. Veitch and his sister were struck several times by bullets, but both survived. Escaping the scene, the men next assaulted a Mr James Dick in Murrayfield at around 8.30 p.m. They presented their revolvers and demanded money, and subsequently pistol whipped him and stole 4s in cash from his person. From there they travelled to Haymarket and took a tramcar through the city. At 9.30 p.m. they committed their third criminal act of the night in Bonnington Road. On this occasion they approached a baker's van driven by one Charles Kenney. Dragging him from his seat, they threw him face down to the ground and sat across him. They demanded his money, which was in a satchel underneath him, to which he clutched tightly and refused to give up. Beginning to cut the strap of the satchel, the assailants were scared off by the cries of someone coming across the scene and fled in the direction of Leith. At midnight they were arrested for loitering near the rear of the Custom House by Police Sergeant Arnot,

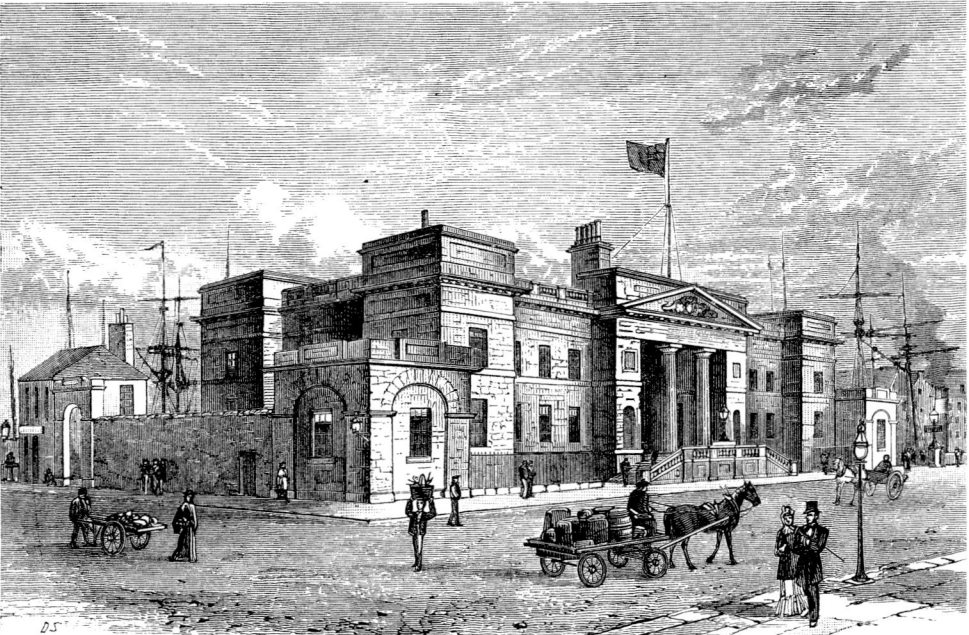

The Custom House in Leith. (Author's Collection)

but as he led them towards the police office one of the men drew his gun and shot the sergeant in the head. Despite his injury, Arnot managed to blow his whistle and other police officers set off in pursuit. A running gun battle ensued, during which two more policemen were shot. One of the assailants, cornered and clearly reasoning that he would soon be out of ammunition, without warning placed the gun in his own mouth and fired through his own brain, falling instantly dead to the ground. The other continued to evade capture, firing indiscriminately at the officers pursuing him until, placing the gun to his own head in a similar fashion to his colleague, he too attempted suicide, but on this occasion the gun misfired and he was taken into custody. The man gave the name James Grant, and that of his deceased companion as Frederick Seymour, although it was believed that both names were assumed. It was thought at the time that the men might have been members of Ned Kelly's gang, on the run after his capture and execution the previous year.

5 FEBRUARY 1828: The West Port Murders

During late January and early February the notorious murderers Burke and Hare took their first two victims. Having discovered the previous November that there was good money to be had from selling the corpses of dead lodgers to the medical schools, they had presumably been waiting for another to fall sick and die so that they could earn a little extra whisky money. The opportunity arose when Hare took in a retired miller named Joseph, who fell ill with a fever. Cholera and typhus being endemic in Edinburgh at this time, the pair justified their next action to themselves with the excuse that Joseph was not long for this world anyway, and that his presence in the house would scare off other customers. So, one night, the pair plied Joseph with whisky until he was insensible, and while in this state one of them lay across his body to prevent any movement while the other placed a pillow over his mouth and nose and suffocated him. His body was transported to Surgeon's Square, where the pair had already made the acquaintance of Dr Alexander Knox and his students. A quick look at the body decided them that it was worth £10, and the pair left happy men. Their next victim was an English street vendor who sold matches and took a bed in Hare's house for a few nights. He had only been there a day or two before he came down with jaundice. Again the pair decided that he most likely would not survive and they would be doing him a service by putting him out of his misery. It would not be long before they ceased to make such excuses, even to themselves.

6 FEBRUARY 1615

Earl Patrick of Orkney, cousin of King James VI and son of James V, was publicly beheaded in the High Street for the crime of usurping the King's authority, by setting himself up as a monarch on those islands and, over the course of twenty years, passing his own laws, collecting taxes and generally behaving as if independent of the Scottish nation. His son, Robert Stuart, had already been executed for organising a rebellion in support of his father.

7 FEBRUARY 1633

George Nicol, the son of an Edinburgh tailor, attended King Charles I in London with accusations against numerous leading figures in the Scottish administration of mismanagement of the treasury. The supposed culprits were summoned to London where it quickly transpired that Nicol did not have the proof to back up his case, and he was returned to his native city in the custody of those he had accused. As punishment he was made to stand at the entry of the session house for an hour, and upon the Mercat Cross for two hours, with a paper on his head reading, 'Here stands Mr George Nicol, who is tried, found, and declared to be a false calumnious liar.' He afterwards received six lashes of the whip across his naked back and was sent to the Tollhouse Gaol.

8 FEBRUARY 1858

The death of John Gray, who worked for Edinburgh City Police as a night watchman, sparked one of the most enduring tales with which the city is associated. Gray died of tuberculosis and was buried in Greyfriars Kirkyard. For the previous two years he had performed his duties, and lived his daily life, in the company of a small Skye terrier he had named Bobby. After his death, Bobby was said to have taken up a post next to his master's grave, and spent every night there from then until his own death fourteen years later. For the first few nights the curator of the graveyard chased him away, but eventually, impressed with his devotion, he allowed him to stay. His story soon spread throughout the city, and local families and shopkeepers brought him food and water. In 1867 Bobby was declared a stray and scheduled for termination, but was rescued from his fate when the presiding Lord Provost of the city, Sir William Chambers, agreed to pay his licensing fees. The story of Greyfriars Bobby has been retold many times, and a statue of the little dog now stands on the corner of Candlemaker Row opposite the entrance to the kirkyard.

The statue of Greyfriars Bobby in Candlemaker Row. (Author's Collection)

9 FEBRUARY 1823

In the very early hours of the morning police were called to 82 South Bridge, a house of ill repute run by a woman named Mary McKinnon. A fracas had broken out between a group of drunken revellers and the girls who plied their trade in the house, which had left one of the men, William Howatt, bleeding on the kitchen floor with a knife wound to the heart – a wound that would claim his life eleven days later. Howatt had been with a group of friends who, after a dinner party at which a considerable quantity of alcohol had been consumed, had decided to go out on the town to continue their revelry. Arriving on the South Bridge they eventually ended up at McKinnon's establishment and had taken a room where they and some of the girls had begun to party. However, some of the men felt uncomfortable, not having realised the nature of the house they were entering, and at some point it was decided to leave, whereupon the girls became angry, feeling that they had not yet emptied the pockets of their guests sufficiently to justify the time spent entertaining them. A squabble broke out which spread to the kitchen, and some of the men managed to depart with the help of a maid, who then went to fetch the mistress of the house who was absent at the time. Returning, she immediately selected a sharp knife with which to threaten the men into good behaviour. In the ensuing moments an altercation occurred between herself and Howatt, and she struck out at him causing the fatal injury. An interesting footnote to this affair is that it was one of the first occasions on which surgical testimony was used to establish guilt in a murder case, the doctors testifying that they had traced the path of the blade through the body and that the blow had been struck downwards, in an offensive rather than a defensive movement. McKinnon's was hanged for the crime on 16 April 1823.

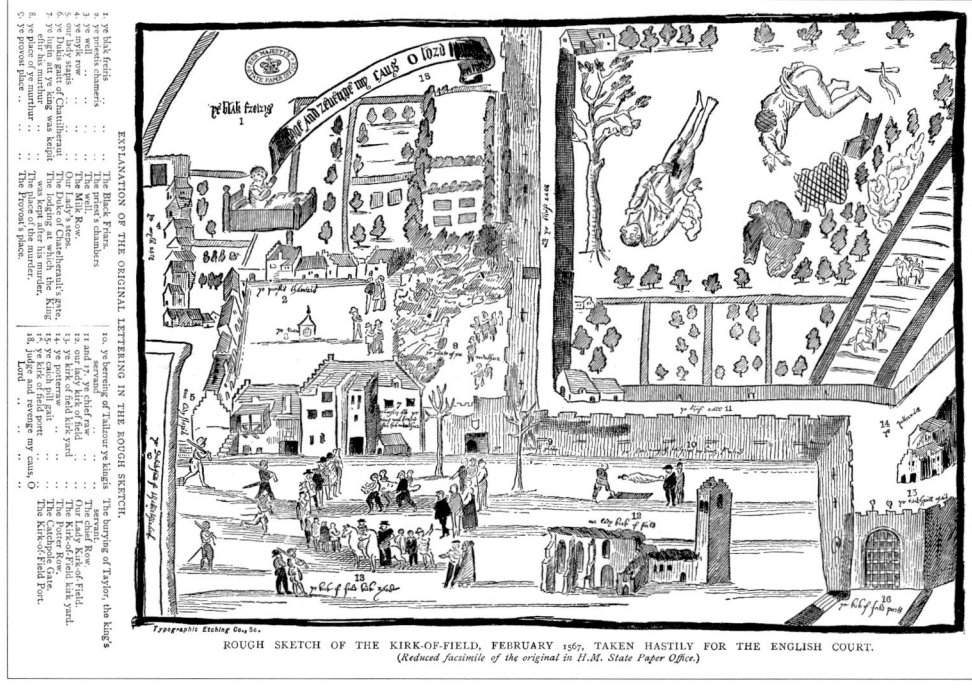

ROUGH SKETCH OF THE KIRK-OF-FIELD, FEBRUARY 1567, TAKEN HASTILY FOR THE ENGLISH COURT.
(Reduced facsimile of the original in H.M. State Paper Office.)

Contemporary sketch of the scene of Lord Darnley's murder, produced for the English court. (Author's Collection)

James Patrick Hepburn, Lord Bothwell.
(Author's Collection)

10 FEBRUARY 1567

An explosion that lit up Edinburgh on the night of 9 February 1567 would herald an event the repercussions of which would last for decades, and possibly even centuries to come. The following morning, in the grounds of the house at Kirk O'Fields in which the explosion had occurred, the body of Henry Stuart, Lord Darnley, husband to Mary Queen of Scots and father to the future King James VI, was found strangled to death. The plot to kill Darnley had been forged by Lord Bothwell, the Queen's senior advisor, most likely without Mary's knowledge, but possibly with her tacit approval. The marriage had been a political one, and from the first Darnley had been a profligate drinker and gambler and had sown his seed widely among the womenfolk of the Scottish capital, and by some accounts the menfolk as well. However, it was his involvement in the murder of David Rizzio that especially enraged his wife. Bothwell and his men had intended to assassinate the consort by the explosives, which were placed in a chamber beneath his bedroom. Darnley, however, was not in his room when the explosion occurred. Hearing the activity of the men below, he had become suspicious and escaped the room with three servants by lowering himself out of the window on a rope. However, he did not escape for long, as he was immediately set on by his assassins and despatched along with one of the servants.

11 FEBRUARY 1653

A person was hanged in Edinburgh on this date for 'irregularities of conduct'. The person in question was most likely an hermaphrodite. Legally a man, but going by the name of Margaret Rannie, he was in the habit of going about the town in women's attire. According to one contemporary journal writer, 'when opened by certain doctors and apothecaries, [he] was found to be two every way, having two hearts, two livers, two every inward thing.' This, of course, is not medically possible, and likely the reference is to the possession of aspects of both male and female sexual organs.

12 FEBRUARY 1828: The West Port Murders

Burke and Hare's third victim, killed on this date, was also the first where they could no longer make excuses for their behaviour. There was no sickness to hide behind on this occasion; the victim, albeit elderly, was in healthy condition. Her name was Abigail Simpson, and she was a widow from Gilmerton who came into Edinburgh on a weekly basis to collect a pension of 1½s and a can of dripping from her former employer. While in the city she would supplement her income selling salt and kaolin. Burke met her hawking in the street and invited her back to Hare's lodging house where they drank together until long into the night. The following morning Abigail, obviously feeling the worse for wear, was persuaded to drink more as a 'hair of the dog', until she was once more insensible. Hare arrived, and together the pair treated her as they had the others, one covering her body while the other closed off her nose and mouth until she ceased to struggle. The body was then undressed and packed in a tea chest ready for delivery to Surgeon's Square.

13 FEBRUARY 1826

William Pollock stood trial on this date accused of stabbing his wife to death at their home in Gifford Park, just outside the city, on 11 November of the previous year. The killing was committed during a bout of excessive violence performed before the couple's 5-year-old son. Although propriety prevented the newspapers from describing the full details of the crime, it seems that the knife had been thrust into the woman's vagina. Pollock was sentenced to be hanged on 22 March. However, the public were to be cheated of their chance to see justice exercised. Two days before the date of execution, Pollock used a portion of his shirt and a strip of blanket to fashion a crude noose, which he attached to his bed and around his neck before throwing himself into a ventilation shaft and ending his own life.

14 FEBRUARY 1911

John Hutchinson, a young chemist from Musselburgh, absconded from justice on this day. Having got himself into debt through speculation, and having had much of his property, including his beloved car, repossessed, he devised a plan whereby he would solve his problems by inheriting his father's property. On 3 February his parents held a party to celebrate their silver wedding anniversary, and as a treat for their guests had bought in some of the finest fresh coffee. Hutchinson was in charge of handing round the cups. Soon after drinking the beverage fifteen of the guests began to show symptoms of a serious sickness, clutching their stomachs, vomiting and wracked by severe pains. Doctors were called, but the father, Charles Hutchinson, and a grocer named Clapperton who had supplied the coffee, were in too serious condition to be saved and passed away within a few hours. Hutchinson was not at first suspected, but as it became obvious that the coffee had been laced with arsenic, a substance he had easy access to in the chemist shop where he worked, and as he had been in charge of the cups at the party, he soon fell under suspicion. The young man left town stating that he was going to stay with friends in Newcastle, but in reality he travelled first to London, and then onwards to Guernsey where he was recognized, but committed suicide by swallowing arsenic himself before he could be arrested.

15 FEBRUARY 1832

During the Middle Ages the greatest health risk to the inhabitants of Edinburgh may have been the plague, but by the nineteenth century it was cholera. On this date the *Scotsman* newspaper reported on the latest outbreak: 'Since our last report, two cases of cholera have terminated fatally. The husband of the woman who died a fortnight ago in Skinner's Close was seized on Saturday and died on Monday in the hospital at Queensbury House. As his age was 83, the fatal issue of the case might have been anticipated. Late on Tuesday evening, another case occurred in the Low Calton. The patient was immediately conveyed to Drummond Street Hospital where he had every attention paid him, but the disease terminated in death this morning. We have just heard that an additional case occurred today in West Register Street, but as it has not been intimated by the Board of Health, the numbers officially reported up to this date stand thus – Total number of cases in Edinburgh since the disease commenced: 13, deaths: 8.'

16 FEBRUARY 1700

Anne, Countess of Wemyss and daughter of 1st Duke of Queensberry, was involved in a horrible accident in Queensberry House in the Canongate. We are told that she accidentally set fire to her 'apron, night-rail and steinkirk. Her nose was burnt off, and her eyes burnt out. Opening her mouth to call, the flame went in and burnt her tongue and throat.' The unfortunate woman died from her injuries.

17 FEBRUARY 1834

The case of Mary Braid, due to be executed on this date until a last minute reprieve was given, was one that shocked Edinburgh society. Braid, from the village of Libberton, had been convicted of murder and carrying on an incestuous relationship with her brother Thomas, with whom she had lived as man and wife for two years. On 10 April of the previous year she had given birth to his child, and in order to conceal this fact had, a few months later, cast the baby into the Union Canal with a rock tied around its neck. Although both were found guilty of incest, the charge of murder against Thomas was found 'not proven', and as such he was sentenced to transportation for life.

18 FEBRUARY 1595

Hercules Stewart, the unfortunate brother of the Earl of Bothwell, by now considered an outlaw, was executed at the Mercat Cross for complicity in his sibling's crimes. This caused an outcry in the city by those who could not believe that he could possibly be involved, having always been a simple and peaceable gentleman. His body was therefore cut down quickly by the crowd and taken to the Tollbooth to be dressed properly for a Christian burial, whereupon it was found that he was not dead and began to revive. Although a deputation was quickly sent to the King to plead for his reprieve, the order had already been given and Stewart was swiftly dispatched by strangulation.

19 FEBRUARY 1829: The West Port Murders – The History of William Burke

Born in County Tyrone, Ireland, in 1792, the son of a respectable Catholic labourer, Burke served in the Army and was married to a woman named Margaret Coleman, by whom he had two children. In 1818 he abandoned his family and came to Scotland to work on the construction of the Union Canal. He laboured on the canal for four years, during which time he fell in with Helen McDougal, a Scotswoman from near Falkirk, who would become his common-law wife and be charged with murder alongside him. After the completion of the canal, he and Helen traipsed around the country performing odd jobs and selling goods in the street. He also learned the trade of a cobbler and made a decent living from it. The couple arrived in Edinburgh in 1827, where Burke's brother Constantine already lived with his family, and late that year they met Maggie Hare, whom Burke had apparently known in Ireland. She enticed them to come and stay at the lodging house she ran with her husband, and the rest, as they say, is history.

William Burke, contemporary trial portrait. (S.P. Evans)

20 FEBRUARY 1650

John Lawson of Leith, having 'by false service' arranged for a house left vacant by the plague to come into the ownership of one who was not entitled to its claim, was found guilty of perjury. For his crime he was bound fast to the Mercat Cross with a paper on his head declaring his crime. His tongue was then drawn from his mouth with a pair of pincers and pierced with a red-hot iron.

21 FEBRUARY 1706

The *Edinburgh Courant* reported that on this date, 'Alexaunder Geddes, one of the Gentlemen of Her Majesty's House Guards, was killed cowardishly by Mr Dunlop, one of the said troop of guards, who has made his escape.'

22 FEBRUARY 1854

A few hours after supporting struts had been removed following the completion of repair works, a large section of the city wall, about 20ft high, which bounded one side of Leith Wynd, collapsed into the alleyway causing tremendous damage to property and burying several people, many of them children, beneath the rubble. In all, three of the children lost their lives, two being killed in the collapse and the other succumbing to head injuries a few days later.

23 FEBRUARY 1950

While lifting a barge from the Union Canal at Redhall, a 10-ton train-mounted crane toppled and crashed into the canal, taking with it two of the plate wagons of the train. Two railway workers who were on the wagons managed to jump clear in time, but Alexander Brown, the crane operator, was trapped under 5ft of water in the upturned cabin, and rescue workers were unable to extricate him before he drowned.

24 FEBRUARY 1729

A report in the *Edinburgh Courant* of this date records that, 'some days ago, died a young man in the parish of Glencorse, who since Saturday last hath been grievously tormented by wicked spirits who haunted his bed almost every night. There was no formed disease upon him; yet he had extraordinary paroxysms, which could not proceed from natural causes. He vomited vast quantities of blood, which was like roasted livers, and at last, with violent cries, his lungs.'

25 FEBRUARY 1697

John Fraser was set at liberty on this day after undergoing a period of penance by order of the Lord Advocate, during which he had to attend in turn all the kirks in Edinburgh dressed in sackcloth and beg public forgiveness until he had been pardoned in each of them. His crime had been that he 'argued against the being of a God, the persons of the Trinity, the immortality of the soul, and the authority of the Scriptures.' A bookseller, he stated in his defence that he had merely been quoting a book in his possession. However, the Lord

Advocate had begun something of a witch hunt against blasphemous publications, including those which promoted 'popery', and the previous year had passed an edict that all booksellers in the capital should provide exact catalogues of all books they had for sale, under penalty that all not listed would be confiscated.

26 FEBRUARY 1925

A report in the *Scotsman* newspaper gives details of a rather unusual kind of suicide. Under normal circumstances one of the clearest indications that a person has taken their own life is the finding of the instrument of their death close at hand. Charles Reid, however, chose to slit his own throat with a razor while standing on the edge of Salisbury Crags and, having done so, either fell or leapt to the pathway below. As such his body was discovered some 120ft below the location where the razor had fallen.

27 FEBRUARY 1610

Lady Amisfield was admitted this day to the Tollbooth Gaol to visit her neighbour, Alexander Kirkpatrick, accused of the murder of James Carmichael. Granted by the keeper of the prison the use of his private apartments for the visit, it was later discovered that the pair had exchanged clothes and that Kirkpatrick had left the prison in her place.

28 FEBRUARY 1769

Mungo Campbell, an officer in the employ of the excise in Ayrshire, hung himself in his cell in the Tollbooth Gaol in the early hours of this morning. He had been found guilty of murder and sentenced to execution the previous day, having accidentally shot the nobleman, Lord Eglinton, during an altercation on the latter man's estate near Ardrossan. Eglinton had demanded his gun, and Campbell replied that he had the right to carry it in his duties and would yield it to no man. The custom being that the bodies of executed men should be handed over to the medical fraternity for dissection, this was arranged, but friends of Campbell's objected, claiming that the same treatment was not prescribed for suicides. Their argument prevailed and they were granted the body, which they buried in unconsecrated ground at the foot of Salisbury Crags. However, the inhabitants of the city, feeling they had been cheated of justice, decided to dig it up again and subject it to the humiliation they felt it deserved. After tossing it between themselves for a while, they took it to the top of the Crags and flung it off. In order to prevent any further indignity, Campbell's friends chose subsequently to have the body buried at sea.

MARCH

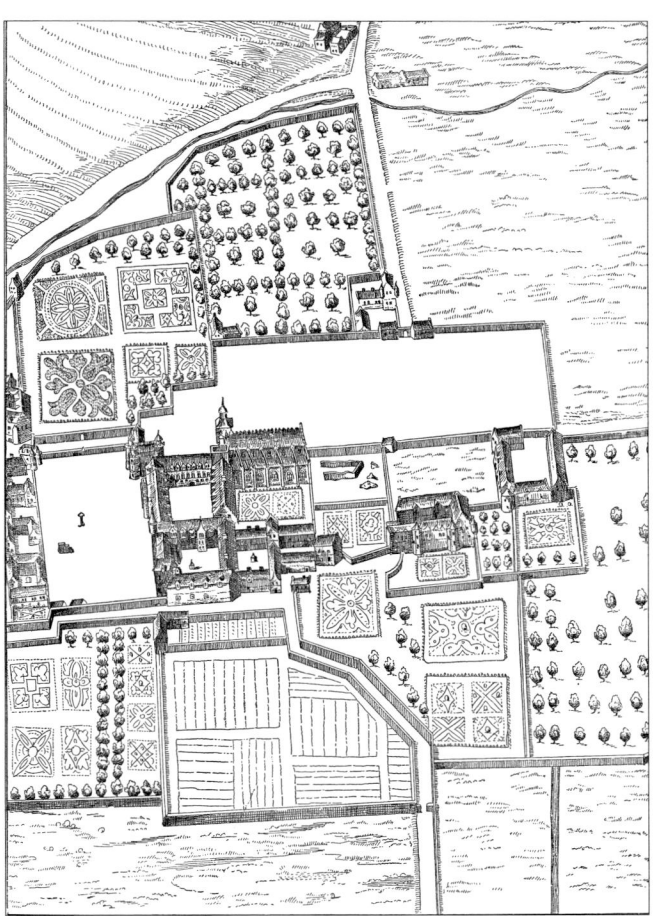

Map of Holyrood Palace, 1647. (Author's Collection)

1 MARCH 1828: The West Port Murders – The History of William Hare

William Hare, contemporary trial portrait. (S.P. Evans)

Like his partner, Hare was also born in Ireland, although in which part is unknown. Also like Burke, and many other Irishmen, he too came to Scotland to work on the Union Canal. On completion of the work he travelled to Edinburgh, where he met a man named Logue and took lodgings with him in Tanner's Close in the West Port, the maze of squalid alleyways and passages at the foot of the Castle Rock. For the next four years he made a living going about the streets with a horse and cart selling fish and scrap. While living there, he began an affair with Logue's Irish common-law wife, Maggie Laird. When Logue died in 1826, Hare married Maggie and took possession of the house, which he continued to run as a lodging house as his predecessor had. Late in 1827, he rented the back room of the house to William Burke and Helen McDougal, and within a few weeks their macabre partnership began.

2 MARCH 1681

Three men by the names of Gogar, Miller and Sangster went willingly to their deaths upon the scaffold as Covenanters rather than submitting to the King's authority. The Duke of York, later King James VII, on hearing of their impending doom, took pity and provided them with a means of escaping their fate. He had the Earl of Roscommon attend the men on the scaffold, and offer that their executions would be reprieved if they would there and then publicly pronounce the words 'God Save the King.' All three refused, stating that they would rather die than accept such terms, and were promptly terminated.

3 MARCH 1732

Joseph Home, a soldier at Edinburgh Castle, was sentenced to death on this date for the murder of a shoemaker named Riddoch. A month earlier, while Riddoch was walking with his wife in St Mary's Wynd, heading for his home in the Pleasance, he fell into an argument with the soldier. The argument escalated into blows, and the fight was said to have continued for upwards of an hour, with local inhabitants struggling to separate the men. Eventually the soldier left, but apparently only to go and fetch his sword, and he reappeared just as Riddoch was about to enter his home. Seeing the soldier, who commenced once again with threats, he rushed at him and the sword was instantly run through his chest. Witnesses were unable to say whether the soldier had intended to stab Riddoch, or whether the victim had run onto the drawn sword, but as there were two wounds and not one it was clear that either way the soldier had withdrawn the sword and then run him through a second time. After several stays of execution he received a remission of sentence in October of the same year.

4 MARCH 1839

When workmen arrived on this Monday morning to resume construction of a bridge for the Newhaven Railway at the end of Warriston Crescent, they found the body of a man floating in a pool of water that had formed in the hole dug for the foundations. The man was said to be poorly dressed and had the appearance of a labourer. However, after being taken to the police mortuary, the body lay unclaimed and unidentified.

5 MARCH 1827

Tried in the High Court of Justiciary on this day were Allan Grant, James Kenny Stewart, Mary Muirhead and Isabella Gray, on a charge of robbery and murder. The two women had met a man named Mark Dow and enticed him back to Stewart's drinking establishment in North Bank Street. There, Muirhead managed to purloin a bill for £42 from his clothing and left, but on finding it missing Dow proposed to follow and mentioned as much to the landlord. The two men, together with Grant who held a torch, went outside, and within a few minutes Dow was found at the foot of the steps to the establishment with his neck dislocated, from which he died shortly after. His clothing and a further £40 in cash had also been removed from him, some of which were found in Grant's apartments. The four were found guilty of the robbery, but as nobody had witnessed the man's fall it could not be ascertained whether or not there was deliberate intent to kill, and the charge of murder was dropped. All four were sentenced to terms of transportation.

6 MARCH 1860

The execution by hanging of Edwin Salt was scheduled for this date until a last-minute commutation was received. Salt had been found guilty of murdering his wife, Mary-Ann, at their home in Juniper Green on the outskirts of the city. The deceased woman had caused her husband no end of trouble through her drunken behaviour and was said to be of dirty habits and neglectful of her four children. On the day before her death she was seen by several people lying insensible on the kitchen floor with blood on her face, and a girl who often came to help the family had put her to bed. The following morning a doctor was fetched and told by the woman that her husband had beaten her. She died later that day, and a post-mortem examination showed that the cause of death was internal bleeding brought on by a blunt instrument, possibly a walking-stick or a fire poker, having been thrust at least eighteen inches deep into her vagina. The doctors were of the opinion that Mr Salt must have done this at a time when his wife was insensible with drink. Salt's defence had insisted that the wounds were self-inflicted; although the doctors called for the prosecution insisted that this was not possible, and even the doctor testifying for the defence admitted that it was unlikely that the woman would have been capable of cleaning an instrument and putting it away after using it in such a way. Salt was convicted by a 10 to 5 majority, and after commutation was committed to prison for life.

7 MARCH 1691

During the reign of William and Mary, a number of French Protestant refugees came to Scotland to escape the Catholic regime of their own country. Three such were the Poiret brothers, George, Isaac and Elias, the latter of whom was known as Le Sieur de la Roche. In Edinburgh they had found employment serving in the King's Scottish Guards, and were on this night staying in the lodging house of John Brown in the Kirkgate of Leith. Also in the house was John Sinclair, a writer, and Sinclair of Mey, who were having a little party in their rooms, to which the Master of Tarbat and an Ensign John Mowat had come to enjoy the revels. During the night, Tarbat took a fancy to a serving girl who brought them their ale. In order to escape his amorous advances, she had bolted to her room and locked herself in, and when the Master followed, he mistakenly ran into the room of George Poiret, followed by Mowat.

Kirkgate of Leith.
(Author's Collection)

Poiret, rudely awakened from his sleep, drew his sword and threatened the men, who quickly set about disarming him. On petition from another servant of the house, the two men retired, giving their apologies to the stricken Frenchman and taking his sword away with them. But in their drunken state, they decided they had not apologised properly and returned to the room to do so. Poiret, alarmed that they might have come back to do him harm, alerted his brothers, sleeping in the room above, by banging on the ceiling with the fire tongs, whereupon they both came down to his room with swords and pistols drawn. The group set to fighting, and within moments Elias Poiret lay dead, run through with a sword. Shortly afterwards Mowat was discovered hiding under an outside stair with his own sword bloodied to the hilt. Brought to the scene, he refused to admit having killed the man and would only state that he wondered who did. Mowat and Tarbat were tried for the murder, together with John Sinclair, but the jury returned the verdict that the crime was 'not proven', and that the killing could only be regarded as part of an unfortunate scuffle arising from intemperance.

8 MARCH 1824

Mary Crocket died on this date in the Royal Infirmary from complications of a knife wound after lingering sixteen days. On 20 February she had been at her home where her daughter, who had left her husband to live with a man named McIntosh, had a meeting with her former spouse, Daniel Elphinstone, at which he had demanded she return to him a Bible and a diamond, and when she refused he had thrown a 14lb weight at her and had taken her scarf away with him. Mrs Crocket then chased Elphinstone down Libberton's Wynd, screaming abuse at him and saying he had turned her daughter into a whore. Then, picking up a barrel she threw it at him. The barrel missed and he picked it up and flung it against a wall before appearing to strike Mrs Crocket in the side. It was only after she returned to her home at the head of the wynd that her husband noticed blood on the side of her dress and she realised that she had been stabbed. Elphinstone, a man said to have been previously of good character, was found guilty of murder and sentenced to be hanged.

9 MARCH 1566

David Rizzio was an Italian-born son of a music teacher who, after coming to Scotland in the train of the Count de Moretto in 1561, ingratiated himself with Mary Queen of Scots through his abilities as a singer and musician. Despite history remembering him as a tremendously ugly man and a flamboyant homosexual, rumour in the court painted him as the Queen's illicit lover when he rose through her ranks to become her private secretary in 1564. Rizzio was ambitious, and it may be that he overstepped his boundaries and attempted to gain too much influence. Resented as both a foreigner and a Catholic, a conspiracy soon grew against him, led by Mary's husband Lord Darnley. On this night, Darnley's band of rebels broke into the Queen's dining room during a meal at which Rizzio was present and demanded

that the man be handed over to them. Rizzio hid behind the Queen, which led to one of the rebels levelling a gun at the monarch herself. News of what was occurring began to travel and men in the city flooded down to Holyrood to aid the royal personage, but were ordered by her to disperse from an upstairs window where the gun was still aimed at her back. A violent struggle then ensued, during the course of which Rizzio was stabbed fifty-seven times and thrown down a staircase, his corpse then being stripped of its jewels and finery by the men before they departed.

The Murder of David Rizzio. (Sir William Allan, 1833.) (Author's Collection)

10 MARCH 1940

Wartime blackouts were intended to save lives, but in the case of art student Peggy McKerlich the blackout on this date had the opposite effect. Walking in the King's Park, she became disoriented by the complete darkness and walked directly off the north end of the Dunsappie Rock. She was conveyed to the Royal Infirmary suffering from fractures to the spine and both legs and died from her injuries three weeks later.

11 MARCH 1889

Jessie King, the notorious 'Stockbridge baby farmer', was executed at the Calton Gaol on this day, the last woman to be hanged in Edinburgh. King was convicted of the murder of two children, with a third strongly suspected. Whether there were others is not known. It was common in those days for a family with a baby which they were unable to bring up themselves – for whatever reason – to offer the baby through advertisement, and pay a good sum of money to the person willing to take the child. The first child taken on by King was a boy named Walter Anderson Campbell. She was paid £5, and in this instance it seems to have been a genuine wish to have a child of her own. However, shortly afterwards her husband returned from work one day to find the child gone, his wife informing him that, unable to cope, she had placed the boy in an orphanage. There are several discrepancies in her story which suggest that this was not the case, however no body was ever found and no charges were forthcoming. From the second baby on it seems obvious that King looked on the matter as simply a financial transaction. The bodies of Alexander Gunn and Violet Tomlinson were both found at the home of King and her husband in Cheyne Street. The first grisly discovery of Alexander was made by some boys, who found a bundle of rags containing what they thought were some old boots to be thrown out and started to kick it around like a football before discovering what was inside. Suspicion quickly fell on Jessie, who had recently made the transaction for the acquisition of Violet, whom she claimed had been sent to a sister who was married to one of the Duke of Montrose's pipers. A search of the house quickly turned up the body, hidden in a coal closet to which only King had the key. She eventually admitted killing the two children, maintaining that both were accidents, and still claiming that young Walter had indeed been sent to an orphanage, although none existed at the address given. Her husband maintained no knowledge of his wife's doings, and fully cooperated with the police in their investigation. Although the defence at King's trial attempted to shift the blame onto him, he does appear to have been entirely innocent.

12 MARCH 1732

A riot broke out at West Kirk, on the outskirts of the city, which left some twelve people severely wounded. The cause of the riot was the reading of an edict naming one Patrick Wedderspoon to be the new minister of the church, a controversial appointment as some of his views were not in accord with those of his parish. On the day the edict was to be read from the pulpit of the church, a great crowd had gathered inside in order to try to dissuade the standing minister from reading it. When the time came for the reading, a great mass of them rushed forward and laid hands on the minister and attempted to take the edict from him. Things quickly got out of hand and Baillie Charles Crockat, who was in attendance, called in the city guard to quell the disturbance even though this was outside of their jurisdiction. Two men were swiftly taken to prison, including the Beadle on the charge that he refused to affix the edict to the church door, although it later transpired that it was not his office to do so. Later, after the riot had been quelled, a second detachment of guard arrived and tried to arrest Mary Campbell, a maidservant in the home of one Mr McVicar, whose household, on trying to prevent the arrest, were all badly beaten. Later still, some boys began to throw stones at the company of the guard, whereupon the soldiers began firing into the crowd of people assembled. In all, eleven were shot, while a twelfth received wounds to the head with a Lochaber axe. Ironically, Mr Wedderspoon's appointment would only last two months, for on 12 May he took a fever and died.

13 MARCH 1662

A young writer by the name of Thomas Hepburn was strangled in his bed, and afterwards a knife thrust through his throat to make sure he was dead. His body being carried into the High Street, it was left next to a midden head (a repository for household waste), where a maid from a nearby home discovered it. On reporting the matter to the guard, five men found drinking in the lodging where he had been killed were arrested, although they strenuously denied the charge.

14 MARCH 1898

Under Scottish law, juries consist of fifteen persons, and a majority verdict is all that is needed to convict. Such was the case with John Herdman, executed on this day after being found

West Kirk. (Author's Collection)

guilty of the murder of a lady friend, Jessie Calder, on New Year's Day. Calder was found in the top-floor flat of a building at 7 Milne Square on the High Street, her head battered almost beyond recognition and stab wounds in her chest. Herdman and Calder had been drinking for much of the two previous days, and he had been heard arguing with the woman in the apartment that day, and was stopped by police when exiting the building. At his trial, a 10 to 5 majority verdict was returned, the remaining five jurors believing that the drink had diminished his capacity for malice aforethought and opting for the lesser charge of culpable homicide. The dispute was thought sufficient to warrant a petition against the death sentence, which was quickly arranged and sent to Lord Balfour of Burleigh, then Secretary of State for Scotland. After examining all the facts the sentence was upheld.

15 MARCH 1935

When Frederick Campbell Baxter appeared before the Sheriff's Court at Edinburgh on this date, accused of the murder of his wife and daughter, a special defence was entered to the effect that Baxter was insane and therefore unable to instruct counsel for his defence. He had, it was argued, been suffering from a mental disorder for some years. Dr David Henderson, Professor of Psychiatry at Edinburgh University, had examined Baxter and found him to be quite delusional and in a highly unsound mental state. In this delusion he had settled on a plan to shelter his wife and child, to whom he was utterly devoted, from his failures in life by placing them in spiritual safekeeping. Inspired by a picture he had seen in a spiritualist magazine depicting two female figures with their arms raised, reaching for the sun, he associated the image with the idea of their trying to reach the light. The murder had been discovered when Baxter himself had rung the police from a telephone box. While officers kept him on the line, the call was traced and a police car despatched to the location. Baxter then led the officers back to his house where the bodies of Jessie Baxter and their 8-year-old daughter Kathleen were found with axe wounds to their heads. Both appeared to have been killed while they slept.

16 MARCH 1833

Following the death of Lord Eldin, a well-known barrister and art collector, his extensive collection was to be auctioned on this date at his home at 16 Picardy Place. Such was the fame of his exquisite taste that a large crowd of patrons arrived to partake of the bidding, and it was during the sale of a particularly fine Teniers that the floor of the drawing room, unable to take their weight, suddenly gave way. The *Caledonian Mercury* described the scene thus: 'From eighty to a hundred persons, ladies as well as gentlemen, were precipitated in one mass into an apartment below, filled with china and articles of virtue. The cries and shrieks, intermingled with exclamations and ejaculations of distress, were heartrending; but what added to the unutterable agony of that awful moment, the density of the cloud of dust, impervious to the rays of light, produced total darkness, diffusing a choking atmosphere which nearly stifled the terrified multitude and in this state of suspense they remained several minutes.' Amazingly there was only one fatality, a banker from Moray Place named Smith, upon whom the hearthstone had fallen, but many more were injured, among them several members of Edinburgh high society.

17 MARCH 1926

Henrietta Sutherland, hired as a maid and cleaner in the home of a Mrs Bertha Merrett at 31 Buckingham Terrace, had just finished laying the table for lunch and was heading back to the kitchen when she heard a gunshot. A moment later Mrs Merrett's son, Donald, ran into the room and informed her that his mother had shot herself. According to his story, the two had been having strong words over financial irregularities in her affairs, when she had pulled out the gun, placed it to her own head and fired. It later transpired that the financial irregularities in question stemmed from an overdraft at the bank run up by her son cashing fraudulent cheques to pay for the services of a female companion. While the police were happy to accept young Donald's story, the woman's relatives were less impressed, particularly as she had told people in the hospital prior to her eventual death on 1 April that she had simply been sitting going through the accounts when she had heard the bang and felt the pain in her head. Eventually, after lengthy detective work by bank officials, Donald Merrett was charged with the murder of his mother. Unfortunately, at the trial, while the prosecution's forensic expert John Glaister argued that his experiments showed that the gun had been fired from farther away than a suicide would indicate, the defence had hired Sir Bernard Spilsbury, probably the most eminent expert of his day, who, notwithstanding that he had carried out his experiments with a different gun, argued that his findings were entirely concordant with Merrett's story. In the end, Merrett was found guilty of passing the false cheques, but on the charge of murder the jury passed the verdict of 'not proven'. This verdict exists nowhere else in the world, and it is a Scottish way of essentially saying, 'we know you did it, now don't do it again.' He was sentenced to twelve months imprisonment. That Merrett was guilty of the murder of his mother is strongly suggested by the mode of his own death in 1954. Merrett committed suicide in exactly the way he had claimed his mother had, by putting a gun to his own head. The circumstances of his self-termination were that the police were then closing in on him after the murder of his wife and mother-in-law in an attempt to inherit money that had been settled on his spouse.

18 MARCH 1751

The notorious Burke and Hare were not the first of the Edinburgh 'resurrectionists' to consider speeding along the demise of their 'product'. Helen Torrence and Jean Waldie, both nurses, had made a decent living from digging up the recently deceased in their care and selling the

No. 31 Buckingham Terrace, location of the death of Bertha Merrett. (Author's Collection)

bodies to keep themselves in drink. However, on one occasion when they had promised some medical students that they would soon provide delivery of a man on whom they were on death watch, their plans were scuppered when the intended subject inconveniently recovered his health. Desperate for a corpse to take the man's place, the pair engaged a woman and her son in conversation in the street and invited them into their home for a drink. While Torrence kept the woman talking, Waldie took the 8-year-old child into another chamber and smothered him with a bed sheet. After selling the body for 2s, the pair were soon apprehended and were executed in the Grassmarket. Although this was the only charge levelled against them, the suspicion was that this was not the first time they had engaged in such a gruesome game.

19 MARCH 1898

The *Scotsman* newspaper today reported the collapse of scaffolding being used in the construction of a new hotel at Waverley station. The structure, 62ft in height and abutting onto the North Bridge, collapsed onto the crowded streets below after being buffeted by 50mph winds. Remarkably there were only three fatalities; John Shanley and James Taylor dying in the initial incident and William Bain succumbing to head injuries a week later.

20 MARCH 1706

Altercations in the streets of Edinburgh were frequent throughout the Middle Ages and into the more enlightened times that followed. On this day, a man named Archibald Houston accosted one Robert Kennedy and his son, Gilbert, as they left their house in Castle Hill and proceeded towards the Cross for a meeting. Houston had been appointed to retrieve some rent arrears owed by Kennedy, and set about him with violent language. Initially attempting to escape the awkward situation, as they approached the Cross, young Gilbert was provoked by the man's language to strike him in the face. A brawl then broke out whereupon, while Kennedy senior began to set about their assailant with a cane, his son drew his sword and ran the man through, causing a fatal wound. The young man fled the city and was declared outlaw, while his father was given only minor punishment for his part in Houston's death.

21 MARCH 1705

At the Edinburgh Assizes of this date, the notorious pirate Captain Thomas Green was brought to justice for the sacking of a ship off the coast of Malabar, India, the murder of its crew and the robbery of its cargo which, together with the ship itself, was later sold. Green stood trial alongside his entire senior crew with the exception of the second mate, John Reynolds, who was said to be ashore at the time of the action. The unnamed ship belonged to the Scottish India Trading Co. and was captained by a man named Drummond. At the conclusion of the trial, Green and his crew were sentenced to be hung in groups of four and five on the shoreline at Leith on consecutive Wednesdays in April. However, two crewmen, immediately on hearing the sentences, made full confessions in return that their lives would be spared, implicating Green in other acts of piracy and also of the murder of a crewman, Thomas Ciers, who had refused to take part in illegal actions. Their confessions also implicated Reynolds, who was re-arrested, while Captain Drummond's wife attempted to take up a civil suit against the pardoned men. In the end, Green was hung alongside John Madder, the first mate, and James Simpson, the gunner, on 11 April. The other crewmen were subject to numerous stays of execution before having their sentences commuted.

22 MARCH 1931

Leaving her two children alone in their tenement apartment in Barony Street while her husband was away, Mrs Murray went across the hallway to speak to a neighbour. While gone, her 5-year-old daughter went looking for her skipping rope under the bed in which her 2-year-old sister, Christine, was sleeping. Finding it too dark to see, she lit a piece of paper from the fire to illuminate the space, but accidentally set fire to the valance on the bed. By the time she had run to fetch her mother the bed was an inferno, and while several of the tenement occupants tried to enter the room to rescue Christine, none were able to get further than the door before being beaten back by the flames. By the time the fire brigade had extinguished the blaze, all that remained of the little girl were charred remains huddled in the corner of the bed.

23 MARCH 1909

Irish farmer John O'Neil appeared at the city court on this day charged with murder. O'Neil had been on the steps of the public lavatory in Tollcross when, suffering from delerium tremens, he had the delusion that he had to avenge the killing of his brother. For some reason, this delusion caused him to grab hold of 6-year-old Frances Demeo who was playing nearby, and dash his head against the railings of the toilet steps before throwing his body down them. Bystanders quickly subdued the man and rushed to the boy's aid, but the injuries to his head were extensive and he died in hospital a few hours later.

24 MARCH 1831

A daring and ingenious robbery of bank funds took place this day on the Glasgow to Edinburgh mail coach. The plan was organised by George Gilchrist, a coaching agent who, through his work, understood the logistics of the fund transfer. The bank strongbox was placed in a compartment at the front of the coach, locked and chained in place. Gilchrist arranged to purchase all of the tickets for the inside of that day's coach, so that other customers would have to sit on top of the coach. He also arranged for one of his co-conspirators to sit on top with a dog on a chain. This man would keep watch to ensure those inside were not disturbed, while the rattling of his dog chain would mask the sound of the bank box chain. Meanwhile Gilchrist, dressed as a woman, and another man, Robert Simpson, went inside the coach and broke through to the front compartment from the inside, breaking open the box and removing its contents – cash and bonds totalling more than £5,000 – using tools concealed in a hatbox. They then disembarked from the coach at a prearranged point where Gilchrist's brother, William, was waiting to take the money and hide it safely. The plan worked perfectly, but loose lips led to Simpson and another conspirator named Morrison being arrested and agreeing to give evidence in return for their freedom. Gilchrist was put on trial alongside his brother and James Brown, the man who had sat atop the coach, but the case against the latter two was adjudged 'not proven'. Gilchrist was found guilty and hanged on 3 August.

25 MARCH 1826

On this date the *Scotsman* newspaper reported that 'the attention of the police was attracted to a public house in Blair Street, kept by a young man of the name of Smith, from the circumstance of the door having remained shut all day. It was deemed advisable therefore to break it open, when, after proceeding through the shop to one of the apartments in the house, they found him suspended from an iron rod that stretched across the door, quite dead. It is supposed, from the deep indentation made in his neck by the rope, that he must have hung several hours. At a short distance from him, on the floor, was a small stool upset, covered by a blanket. A Bible also was found on the shop counter.'

26 MARCH 1437

When Walter Stewart, the 4th Earl of Athol, tried to seize the crown of Scotland through the attempted assassination of King James I, his punishment was anything but swift. The full sentence was that he was to be publicly tortured for a full three days leading up to the execution as a deterrent to any who might have designs of their own on the monarchy. On the first day he was attached by the arms and legs to a tall crane, from which his body was repeatedly dropped then jerked to a stop before hitting the ground. The result of this was to dislocate virtually every joint in his body. Then, at the Mercat Cross, he was placed in a pillory and a red-hot crown bearing the inscription 'King of All Traitors' was placed on his head where it immediately seared itself into his skin. After being allowed to cool it was ripped back off, taking much of his scalp with it. The second day of punishment consisted of his being dragged naked through the streets of the city while tied to a hurdle pulled by a horse. There are also reports of his being tortured with red-hot pincers on this day, but there is no confirmed reference to this. On the final day, tied to the Mercat Cross, his belly was slit open and his intestines slowly wound on a wooden spindle, while buckets of water were thrown in his face to keep him conscious. After this full disembowelment, his entrails were burned before his eyes before the executioner reached upwards from the now empty abdominal cavity, tore out his still beating heart, and threw this too into the flames.

The Mercat Cross. (Author's Collection)

27 MARCH 1811

Adam Lyall was publicly executed by hanging on this date for the crime of highway robbery. Lyall and his brother John had held up a man named Mathew Boyd on the Sheriffmuir, near Dunblane, the previous October. Levelling their pistols at the man they had ordered him to empty out his jacket and had been rewarded with over £126, a small fortune for that time. Boyd, however, was a clever and resourceful victim and, after being ordered to ride off, had managed to double back and observe the direction of the men's departure. Then, proceeding to Sterling, he obtained a warrant for their arrest and pursued them all the way to Edinburgh, where he eventually apprehended them in Princes' Street. John Lyall, however, was found at trial to be a simpleton and incapable of knowing right from wrong, and as such it fell to his brother to accept the full punishment of law.

28 MARCH 1839

Epidemics of fever have been a constant problem in Edinburgh. In this month, an anonymous correspondent to the Lord Provost gave a reasonable explanation of the cause. 'It has been generally received opinion that a town surrounded by marshes is unhealthy; and, acting upon this opinion, we find the rulers of cities in every quarter of the globe endeavouring to improve the health of the towns by removing the marshes. In Edinburgh, whether the contrary opinion exists or not, an opposite practice at least prevails, and so far from any attempts being made to diminish this source of disease, additions are yearly making to the marshes in the immediate neighbourhood of the town; and, be it remarked, the Edinburgh marshes are no ordinary or natural marshes, where the evaporation is only for a short period of the year, and the effluvia only from simple stagnant water. No, the Edinburgh marshes are artificial, they are made from the irrigation of the ground by the water and filth of the common sewers of Edinburgh; and that which should be carefully conveyed underground to the sea, is at our very doors, and under our very noses, most scientifically spread out and evaporated, to the suffering of thousands.'

29 MARCH 1625

A storm, the like of which had not been seen before in living memory, raged up and down the Firth of Forth, destroying a great deal of shipping and flooding many harbours. The waters rose above the harbour wall in Leith and ran into the houses of the port, rising so high that the boats of the harbour floated inshore and wrecked themselves against the sides of buildings. Two ships masters, James Langlands and Robert Bury, were killed trying to rescue their ships from the tempest, and many other mariners injured as they desperately tried to cast off and put out to sea to escape the squalls. The storm being taken as a bad omen by the superstitious inhabitants of Edinburgh, their fears were confirmed when the following day news was received from London that King James VI (and I of England) had died on 27 March.

30 MARCH 1723

A lady by the name of Elizabeth Murray, wife to a merchant named Thomas Kincaid, was found brutally murdered on the road from Edinburgh to Gogar-Mains. Suspicion for the act having fallen on her husband, he absconded to Holland to escape justice. A published elegy contains the following epitaph:

Here lies inter'd,
A lady in her Prime of Age,
Found reeking in her Gore,
Slain by a Tygar Husband's Rage,
Whose Death all Men deplore.

31 MARCH 1689

In a court case the previous year, a man named John Chiesley of Dalry House divorced his wife, and the presiding judge, Sir George Lockhart, President of the Sessions, awarded her the sum of £93 per year from his estate to care for their eleven children. Chiesley was angered at this, wanting to control the finances of her household himself, and wrote a letter from London to Lockhart warning him that if he did not put things to rights then he would pay with his life. Others heard him threaten likewise, but nobody had taken him seriously. On this date he arrived back in Edinburgh from London, loaded his pistols and took them with him to services at St Giles' Cathedral. From there he dogged Lockhart's footsteps home and shot him in the back as he was about to enter his house. The bullet passed through Lockhart's chest, emerging from the front, and by the time he had been carried inside the house he was dead. Chiesley was instantly seized, and would only say in his defence that, 'I am not wont to do things by halves, and now I have taught the President how to do justice.' He was sentenced to death the following day, as was the custom at the time for those taken red-handed in the act, and the sentence was carried out without further ado. He was dragged on a hurdle to the Mercat Cross, and there his right hand was struck off while still alive, and then he was hanged, and his body hung in chains on the Leith road, while the hand was nailed to the West Port. The body was later stolen at night by his relatives and was said to have been taken

Above: *Dalry House. (Author's Collection)*

Left: *Sir George Lockhart. (Author's Collection)*

back to Dalry House. Thereafter his spirit was reputed to haunt the house, and servants would refuse to enter the back kitchen alone at night. There have been several stories since of a one-armed skeleton being found in various locations around the site of the house.

APRIL

A doorway in Mary King's Close.
(The Real Mary King's Close visitor attraction)

1 APRIL, 1840

The jury in the case of James Wemyss composed a letter to the Queen on this day requesting a stay of execution for the condemned man. This was their second request; the first, a plea for clemency, had been refused. Now they wrote again asking for more time for doctors to investigate the possibility that the murder victim, Wemyss' wife, had had a pre-existing medical condition which may have contributed to her death. During a row in their lodgings, Wemyss had thrown the woman down the stairs and later bashed her head on the fireplace in full view of their fellow lodgers. A stay of ten day was given from the original execution date of 6 April. However, this was merely to be a brief respite, and Wemyss went to his doom on the newly appointed date.

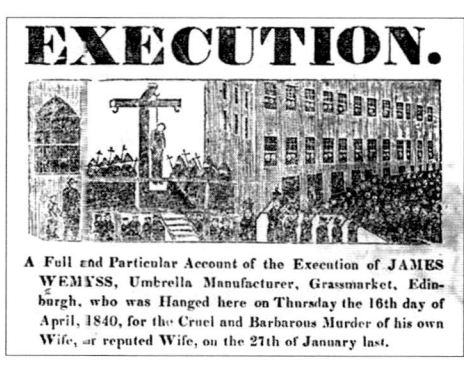

Detail from a broadside regarding the execution of James Wemyss. (Author's Collection)

2 APRIL, 1601

James Wauchope was killed in single combat by Robert Auchmuty, a barber, on St Leonards Hill. Placed in the Tollbooth Gaol, Auchmuty complained of a sickness which rendered him susceptible to light, and as a consequence cloaks were hung over the cell window, both outside and in. In reality the cloaks were hiding the fact that he had nitric acid eating through the bars of the window. Once the bars were gone he attempted to escape, but an all-clear signal given by a servant boy was spotted by a guard and Auchmuty was apprehended, and beheaded ten days later.

3 APRIL, 1683

The funeral was held on this date in Haddington of the Duke of Lauderdale. As per the tradition of the day, after the procession to the church dole money was thrown to the beggars, whereupon one, named Bell, in an attempt to gain more than his fair share of the money, stabbed another. Having been apprehended, he was made to touch the body of his victim, there being a superstition that fresh blood would flow from a corpse when touched by the person who killed him. The blood being observed, the man was declared guilty on the spot, and was hung from the town bridge the following day.

4 APRIL, 1836

Charles Donaldson was hanged on this date for the murder of his wife, Margaret, in Tollbooth Wynd, Leith, the previous November. Although admitting to having killed the woman, Donaldson's defence was that he beat her on a daily basis, often with a frying pan, on account of her drinking habits, and that on the day in question he had not intended to kill her but merely to dole out her daily dose of punishment.

Tollbooth Wynd in Leith.
(Author's Collection)

5 APRIL: Medieval Edinburgh

In the narrow wynds and closes of old Edinburgh, the height of your standing in society could be measured vertically in a literal sense. The narrow confines of the city meaning that most buildings were at least seven and sometimes as many as fourteen storeys high, even the richest folk tended to share a building with several other families. It was your position in the street, and in the building, which spoke of your prestige. The best families lived at the head of the close, usually around halfway up the building. As you went further down, so the better-off folk, the artisans and officials, would live higher up in the very top storeys. Generally, nobody of any note lived further than halfway down the close. There were two reasons for this. The first was light. The narrowness of the closes meant that often they were just wide enough for two people to pass. And with the height of the buildings, light did not penetrate as far as the ground floors except briefly when the sun was directly overhead. Those on the bottom storeys were essentially living in perpetual gloom. But worse than this was the condition of the streets. With no sanitation system, they could often be little better than running sewers, particularly towards the bottom of the close where more and more effluence joined the stream, and so the higher your abode, the less the smell penetrated it.

6 APRIL, 1973

Douglas Knowles was arrested on this date on a charge of murder and theft after an exhaustive enquiry. On 28 February he walked into a betting shop at 31 Slateford Road, concealing about himself a claw hammer. Writing out a slip for a £1 bet on a Hibernian's football match, he approached the counter and, as the proprietor examined the slip, bludgeoned him to death before helping himself to £568 of takings behind the counter. The exact time of the murder was ascertained by others in the building hearing suspicious noises and remembering a news report which had been on the television at the time. The police discovered a betting slip from that precise time that contained distinctive handwriting. Gathering in around 25,000 betting slips from that shop and seven other betting shops in the area, they eventually found a number of slips with the same handwriting, and matched them up to their author. Furthermore,

One of Edinburgh's narrow closes.
(Author's Collection)

they found the murder weapon, which they tied to the crime because it was wrapped in the roller towel from the betting shop's washroom. It was also wrapped with a distinctive hand-embroidered handkerchief, one of a very limited set that Knowles had inherited from an aunt in Northern Ireland. He was sent to prison for life.

7 APRIL, 1932

John Robertson was an unmarried 33-year-old man living with his parents at 17 George Terrace, Blackburn, West Lothian when, on this date, he took an axe and split his mother's head open. Making no attempt to evade capture he was said to appear entirely unconcerned when charged with the crime. His father explained that he had been acting in a progressively strange manner since he had returned from Australia a year and a half previously, had been of a withdrawn nature and frequently had paranoid delusions that people were talking about him. Three medical practitioners who examined him concurred that he was not of fit mental capacity to stand trial and he was remanded in a mental institution at His Majesty's pleasure.

8 APRIL, 1728

From a report in the *Edinburgh Evening Courant*: 'Tony Astons elder and younger, stage players, were committed prisoners to the Tollbooth; 'tis said they are charged with the crime of carrying off a young lady, designed for a wife to the latter.'

9 APRIL, 1670

Of all the witchcraft trials in Edinburgh, none was more notorious than that held on this date of Major Thomas Weir and his sister Jean. One of the most prominent citizens of the city, Major Weir was known as an heroic soldier and Covenanter, and a devout preacher. He had been captain of the town guard, and now was a leading light in the Presbyterian community, attending regular religious meetings and preaching the gospel, and was never

Major Weir's home in the West Bow. (Author's Collection)

seen without the presence of his trusty staff. Then one day, at the age of 70, he stood up in the middle of one of the religious services and began to confess to an astonishing list of crimes, including devil worship, bestiality, and a lifelong incestuous sexual relationship with Jean. At first his friends and neighbours refused to believe it, but eventually his sister confessed that all was true, and the pair were arrested and sent to trial. Jean testified to a natural talent for witchcraft, inherited, she said, from her mother, which she practiced under the name of Grizel. She further confessed that her brother bore the mark of Satan on his body, and that his staff had been given him by the devil himself and was the source of all his power. The pair were sentenced to death. Thomas was taken to the Leith boundary where he was strangled and burned at the stake. When instructed to ask the Lord's forgiveness prior to sentence being carried out, he replied, 'let me alone, I have lived as a beast and I must die as a beast.' Grizel was equally unrepentant and was said to have torn all her clothes off on the gallows and had to be hanged naked. Remembered as the Wizard of the West Bow, Thomas's house was said to be haunted by his spirit and remained empty for over 100 years after his death.

10 APRIL 1645

Records of the Town Council show that on this date Dr Joannes Paulitius, MD, was engaged at a salary of £80 per month to tend to those infected by the plague. This marks the first official record of the last great outbreak of plague in Edinburgh. Paulitius himself fell victim to the plague in June of that year and was succeeded in the role by George Rae, who was offered a very large recompense for taking on the job. Rae survived, and spent the next ten years chasing the money he had been promised. He eventually won his case and was granted an annual pension of £1,200, a fortune at the time. For his bravery, it was no more than he deserved. The 1645 plague outbreak appears to have been of the Bubonic variety, which is transmitted through infection of the blood, usually when the victim is bitten by an infected flea. In this outbreak, the infected were instructed either to remain within their houses and quarantine themselves, or to remove themselves to the Royal Park. A later edict instructed that those who died in the park should be buried there and not in a kirkyard, for fear of transporting the disease, and also from fear that should the graves be reopened later in burying others, that the plague might break out again from the corpses of the infected. Other regulations were established

A plague doctor's outfit similar to the one Dr George Rae would have worn. (Author's Collection)

restricting travel within the country, and stating that nobody should entertain a stranger within their homes without strict permission from the authorities. While Paulitius made little headway with treatment of the disease, Rae seems to have come up with an effective, if somewhat gruesome treatment. Clothing himself head to foot in leather, which probably saved his life as it prevented the fleas from biting through to his skin, and with a beak-like mask filled with herbs to filter the air, he visited the infected and carried out his radical cure. Bubonic plague caused large pus-filled boils to form on the skin, and when these burst the pus entered the victim's blood, causing poisoning and death. Rae's treatment was to slice the tops from these buboes, as they were called, allowing the pus to escape, and to ram a red-hot poker into the wound to quickly cauterise it and prevent the pus from reaching the bloodstream. This was done, of course, in the years before any kind of anaesthetic was available.

11 APRIL, 1574

Robert Drummond, known locally as Dr Handie, having been twice found guilty of adultery, was placed in the stocks at the Mercat Cross, and afterwards was to be branded on the cheek. As this latter punishment was in the process of being prepared, he took up his own knife in front of an assembled crowd and stabbed himself three or four times in the heart.

12 APRIL, 1828: The West Port Murders

On this date Burke and Hare carried out a murder which would be part of their undoing. Mary Paterson was a well-known local prostitute recognised by many for her striking good looks, far in excess of others of her class. William Burke met her, along with another prostitute named Janet Brown, while drinking in William Swanston's grog shop in the Canongate. The two girls had just been released from the watch house, where they had been detained for disturbing the peace. Burke bought them drinks and invited them to breakfast with him. He took them to his brother Constantine's house in nearby Gibb's Close where he claimed to be lodging. They ate their meal and set to drinking whisky, and before long Mary was insensible, but Janet held her liquor better and proved harder to intoxicate. He took her out for a walk and more drink, but when he returned his wife had arrived and an argument ensued, after which Janet left. Hare arrived, together with his wife, and the women were told to wait outside while the two men despatched Mary in their usual manner. Later, Janet returned to collect Mary, to be told by Hare that she had gone out for a walk with Burke, and was invited to wait with him and have a drink. However, fate intervened again, and a servant girl from her lodgings arrived to take Janet back with her before another murder could occur. Later still Janet returned again, but was sent away by Constantine's wife without entering. When the true events of that day became public knowledge, she must have been acutely aware of how close she had come to becoming a victim herself on three separate occasions. Later that night Mary's body was taken to Dr Knox's rooms, where it was instantly recognised by one of his assistants. Burke made an excuse that they had bought it from an old woman who said that the girl had killed herself with drink. A few days later, Knox's doorman David Paterson (no relation to the deceased) asked again where they had obtained her body, and Burke changed his story, replying that he had bought it from friends of the deceased. When Paterson challenged him on this, he threatened to stop providing them with bodies if he continued to ask questions.

13 APRIL, 1682

On this day a complaint was heard before the Privy Council from a servant girl, Janet Stewart, who had been induced into accepting a tablet in the form of a sweet by one Mistress Elizabeth Edmondstoun for the amusement of several guests. The tablet had been created by an Edinburgh apothecary named James Aikenhead, and was said to produce 'strange wanton affections and humours in the bodies of women.' However, the tablet turned out not to have the desired effect, and young Janet fell into a fever lasting twenty days and which left her in such a weak condition that she was thought likely never to fully recover.

14 APRIL, 1736

On 9 January of this year a robbery had taken place in the village of Pittenweem on the Fife coast, the house of an exciseman being burgled and some £200 and goods stolen. Five men were quickly arrested for the crime and three were put on trial. Andrew Wilson, George Robertson and William Hall were found guilty on 2 March, and sentenced to be hung on this date. In the meantime, Hall was reprieved and his sentence commuted to transportation for life. Wilson and Robertson, awaiting their sentence, made an attempt to escape by widening the prison bars and squeezing through, but Wilson, having insisted on going first, and being the bigger of the two men, became stuck in the bars and the plan failed. Feeling guilty because he had prevented his co-conspirator's escape, Wilson pledged that Robertson would not die, and on the Sunday before the execution was due, when the pair were taken to church as was the custom, he seized the guards with his hands and teeth and held them for long enough to allow the other man to abscond. The action found favour with the populace who saw that there was indeed 'honour among thieves', and there was an outcry for his life to be spared. Apprehensive that an attempt at rescue would take place, Captain Porteous of the town guard applied extra security measures for the execution. The hanging itself went off without a hitch, but as the hangman began to cut down the body a riot broke out, and many present began to pelt him with rocks and stones, forcing him to take refuge behind Porteous's guard. On seeing this, Porteous acted rashly and, taking up a musket, fired injudiciously into the crowd, exhorting his men to do likewise. The result was carnage. By the end of the fusillade six lay dead and nine others were wounded. Porteous was immediately arrested by the magistrates on the grounds that they had not ordered his action, and charged with murder.

15 APRIL, 1819

When some young workmen started amusing themselves with jumping games on the main road to Haddington, they were approached by a millwright named Peter Bowers who asked to join in their exertions. Declaring that he could beat any of them in the game, and making a *2d* wager on the matter he refused to pay after losing the bet. He was then challenged by an elderly man named John Sandilands, who said he would jump with him, or fight with him, old as he was, for any wager he liked. An argument then broke out between the two, whereupon Bowers took up an axe he carried with him and struck the older man on the head, breaking open his skull to the extent that brain matter was hanging out and he died shortly after. Bowers was sentenced to death, but later reprieved.

16 APRIL, 1790

In a bizarre example of how quickly a small matter can get out of hand, Sir George Ramsay died this day having been mortally wounded two days earlier in a duel with a Captain Macrae. The latter gentleman had, the previous week, been escorting a lady from the theatre when he attempted to obtain a chair for her, the most common form of public transport in the city at that time. Inquiring of a passing chair if they were free for business, they agreed and he held it ready, but as he did so, a drunken servant grabbed hold of the chair claiming it had been reserved for his mistress. When it transpired that the man's mistress was nowhere to be found, Macrae beat the man with his stick to drive him off. The servant, it turned out, was in the employ of Lady Ramsay, and Macrae, feeling that he had been a little impertinent, attempted to apologise to the lady for so misusing her man, going on his knees to her as she posed for a portrait for Henry Raeburn. She passed the matter off to her husband, who agreed to accept the apology on condition Macrae also apologised for letters demanding the dismissal of the servant. This, on the advice of friends, he refused to do, and the matter ended on the beach at Leith where Ramsay, firing first, grazed Macrae's collar with his bullet. Macrae, out of deference for the wrong he felt he had done the other man, had been intending to fire his bullet in the air, but when he realised that Ramsay had actually attempted to kill him, levelled his gun, took careful aim, and brought the man's life to an end.

17 APRIL, 1935

When Robert Forrest and Adam Shaw entered one of the kilns at Steele Bros enamel works in Portobello to fix up electric lamps in readiness for night work, they little suspected that it would be the last thing they would ever do. Five minutes later the plant manager approached the kiln to wind the clocks that register the heat inside and saw the two men lying unconscious on the floor: they had apparently been overcome by gas fumes released inside the kiln. Although steps were taken to quickly recover them from their position, they were found to be dead a few minutes later.

18 APRIL, 1826

James Hunter, a cowfeeder from Edinburgh, was on his way home from the Lauder Fair in the company of two young ladies he had met along the way when, at just before midnight, the trio passed three men on the road. A moment after they had passed Hunter felt himself tripped from behind and then struck a blow on the head. Falling to the ground, one of the men lay on top of him while another began to rifle his pockets, relieving him of around £11 in bank notes and some change. The women, threatened by the men with the same treatment if they interfered, ran off and gained assistance from a nearby farmhouse, but by the time they had returned the men had left and Hunter had been unable to give chase. Two men, Andrew Fullarton and James Renton, were apprehended and put on trial after they were seen that night in the company of another man named Reid spending a great deal of money in similar denominations and drawn on the same banks. A verdict of 'not proven' was returned against Renton, but Fullarton was found guilty and executed on 16 August.

19 APRIL, 1933

Fifty-three-year-old chartered accountant William Smith Dickison took his own life on this day on the Braid Hills golf course. He was found with a bullet wound in his head, and the revolver lying nearby. He was said to have been suffering from nervous depression due to ill health for the previous two years.

20 APRIL, 1779

The wearing of the kilt has always been a serious business in the Highlands of Scotland, and on this day it became a serious business in Edinburgh as well. Seventy men of the 42nd and 71st regiments, highlanders all, had been marched to Leith to be shipped to India, but a rumour spread that they were to join the Lowland Corps there, and would be forced to dress in a trousered uniform. Swearing to fight this to the death, they encamped on the shore and refused to budge. Two hundred Fencible troops were sent to take them into custody, and Major Sir James Johnston, in charge of the battalion, ordered them to surrender, his words being translated into Gaelic for their understanding. As he did so, a scuffle broke out and one of the Fencibles was bayoneted, whereupon shots were fired, and within minutes the two sides were exchanging fusillades. Two Fencibles were killed, and up to fifty of the highlanders were either slain during the battle or died later of their wounds.

21 APRIL, 1793

At around 3 a.m. an attempt was made to escape from the Tollbooth Gaol. Two men, both awaiting trial on charges of housebreaking and robbery, managed to loosen the hinges to the door of their cell and remove them. Taking the metal thus obtained, they succeeded in making their way to the east end of the prison where they used the nails and other metal materials to scrape away the mortar holding one of the large stones in place. Unfortunately, in doing so, the stone fell outwards from the wall and crashed through the roof of a glover's shop on the other side, causing such a great noise that the whole neighbourhood was alerted and the men were swiftly apprehended. The men, John Stirling and Peter Campbell, were later to plead guilty to all charges and were transported for life.

22 APRIL, 1911

A dramatic attempted rescue of a man on Samson's Ribs came to naught when John Bellinger, a 40-year-old packer, fell to his death on this date. He had descended a niche from the ridge top looking for bird's nests when the ground began to give way beneath him. Two park rangers and two shepherds attempted to prevent his fall. One of the shepherds stretched himself on the cliff top and succeeded in grasping the man's coat collar, while ropes were procured and the second shepherd descended and managed to tie a rope around the man's waist. But when they attempted to pull him up, the rope gave way and he fell to the roadway below, fracturing his skull and his leg. He died without regaining consciousness.

23 APRIL, 1913

Poisoning is a common method used in domestic murder. But sometimes what appears to be a clear-cut case turns out to be nothing of the sort. Such was true on this date when John Saunders, a gamekeeper from East Lothian, was put on trial for the attempted murder of his wife by strychnine poisoning. The pair had been married for twelve years, and Elizabeth Saunders had, all that time, been of a delicate disposition. They lived in a lodge on the estate of Gosford House, which he managed, in a two-bedroom property whereby Elizabeth shared one bedroom with her elderly mother and 21-year-old niece, while her husband occupied the other. It seemed that sexual relations between them were intermittent, and although John Saunders was eager for children, this had not come about. In January of 1913, Mrs Saunders became ill to the point that doctors were called, and she vomited white foamy substances witnessed by others on several occasions. Elizabeth also complained of her food tasting bitter, and her niece tasted the food and confirmed this. Often she had seen a white powder sprinkled on the food, as had others in the household. Eventually it was taken away and tested and found to be the poison in question. It seemed to be an open and shut case: Saunders, tiring of his high-maintenance wife, who would not bear him offspring or share his bed, had decided to do away with her, presumably as a prelude to finding a more accommodating spouse. The problem was that there was no record of John Saunders ever obtaining strychnine, this despite the fact that it was a substance that would be natural for him to possess as he went about his daily business. Furthermore, the poisoning itself was so blatant and obvious that it seemed unlikely that an intelligent man would have incriminated himself so easily. Here was where the psychiatrists became involved. After the prosecution had built its case, the defence set up the alternative scenario whereby Mrs Saunders, in the diminished mental state she had always displayed, and suffering from hysteria, had poisoned herself as an attention-seeking device. Other doctors pointed out that some of the symptoms she had displayed were not actually commensurate with strychnine poisoning, and suggested that there may have been some play-acting involved. By the end of the trial, the defence witnesses had all but destroyed Mrs Saunders credibility, and her husband was quickly found to be not guilty. He shortly thereafter divorced his wife for desertion.

24 APRIL, 1936

Lawrence Wright Kivlin was described as a disturbed youth who was not in his right mind when he assaulted 73-year-old Williamina Gardner at her home at 124 Holyrood Road. He struck her on the head with a wooden block before throwing her to the ground, kicking her about the head and body and cutting her neck and arms with a razor. Pleading guilty to the charge of attempted murder he was sentenced to seven years' penal servitude.

25 APRIL, 1690

The opprobrium and public humiliation brought on a woman giving birth out of wedlock in these times often had drastic results. Rather than bear the shame of performing visible penance for sins, pregnancies were often disguised and the resulting babies quietly disposed of. To counter this problem, the Parliament in Edinburgh passed a law on this day that any woman found to have acted in a secretive manner with regard to a pregnancy, and who did not call for assistance with the birth, and whose baby was now missing or found to be dead, was to be treated as a murderer and sentenced accordingly.

26 APRIL: Resurrectionists

Burke and Hare were not literally bodysnatchers. But many were. Indeed, it was a busy industry, to the extent that many families, on burying their loved ones, would take it in turns to stand guard over the grave each night until such time had passed as to render the body useless. The reason was that until the Anatomy Act of 1832, the only legal supply of corpses for dissection in medical schools was of those condemned to death. And as medical science advanced, and less and less executions took place, the supply had become vastly insufficient. The schools needed bodies, and with no refrigeration facilities, they needed them fresh and were willing to pay. Edinburgh was the centre of activity, most of the big medical schools being located there, so not only were none of the city's graveyards a safe place to bury your dead, but a brisk trade was carried on in importing the stolen dead from other parts of the country. The technique generally used by the grave robbers was to dig down diagonally from above the grave, break open the top end of the coffin, place a rope around the corpse and haul it out. This would mean that the earth above the coffin remained undisturbed and the family would often be none the wiser. The body was then stripped of all clothes, jewellery and other possessions, and these were placed back inside the coffin before the body was taken for sale. This was important, as these items were considered part of the deceased person's estate, and therefore the property of his inheritors, whereas the body itself legally belonged to nobody. As such, being caught in possession of a corpse was a misdemeanour, and punishable with a fine or a short imprisonment, whereas theft of property was a felony and could lead to transportation or even death.

Graves in Greyfriar's Kirkyard. (Author's Collection)

27 APRIL, 1601

Archibald Cornwall, an officer of the town, was hanged at the Mercat Cross and his body hung on a gibbet for 24-hours for burglary and committing a grievous insult to the King and Queen. His crime was to break into a house, possibly of a close associate of the King, and steal images of the monarch and his bride. These he then took to the Cross, where he nailed them to the gibbet as a gesture of his contempt to their persons. The gibbet on which the portraits had been hung was burned, having been in itself rendered insulting by this 'profanity'.

28 APRIL, 1717

Robert Irving, a chaplain who had been employed by wealthy James Gordon as tutor to his two sons, John and Alexander, had, while in this employ, become enamoured of a servant girl in the house and attempted to take liberties with her, to which she objected. The two boys, seeing this act, reported it to their father who reprimanded his employee for his behaviour. An apology was given, but Irving was also noted to have fallen into a melancholy mood afterwards. This day, being a Sunday, Mr and Mrs Gordon went into the city to spend time with friends, taking their daughter with them and leaving their sons in Mr Irving's care. Irving, after giving the boys their lessons, sent them out for a walk, telling them to go via Multrees Hill. They had not long set out when he caught up with them, and shortly afterwards, as they neared Stockbridge, he sat down and told them to play, which they did, gathering flowers and chasing butterflies. After a while he called them to him and remonstrated with them for informing on him. Then he told them he was sorry, but they must suffer for their act and, seizing John, he laid him on the ground, pulled out a pocketknife and cut his throat across. Alexander turned and ran off, but Irving quickly caught up to him and handed out the same treatment. A gentleman out for a walk witnessed the attack from a distance and quickly raised the alarm. Irving meanwhile attempted to cut his own throat and, failing to do so, ran down to the Waters of Leith and threw himself in, with a plan to drown himself. He was dragged from the water, and taken on a cart to the Calton Gaol where he was chained to the floor in the manner of a wild dog. Within two days he appeared before a judge who, given that he was witnessed in the act of the murder, summarily sentenced him to be hanged, and a day later the sentence was carried out.

A view down the excavated Mary King's Close.
(The Real Mary King's Close Visitor Attraction)

29 APRIL 1645

One story of the plague that persists to this day concerns a lane by the name of Mary King's Close, now the site of one of Edinburgh's leading tourist attractions. According to legend, the plague was so persistent in this particular lane that the Town Council took the decision to wall up the ends of the close and leave around 400 inhabitants inside to die, either from the disease or from starvation and dehydration, whichever occurred first. The story, while still appearing in print frequently, has no basis in fact and probably stems from the fact that the close was, a hundred years later, buried in the foundations of the new Royal Exchange building. The plague mostly came to an end in Edinburgh in November of that year when a tremendous two-day rainstorm washed out the streets and closes, drowning many of the rats who carried the plague fleas.

30 APRIL 1520

A skirmish which became known as 'Cleanse the Causeway' took place on this day on the streets of the city. The main protagonists were Archibald Douglas, 6th Earl of Angus, and James Hamilton, 1st Earl of Arran. The fight was precipitated by Angus' marriage to Margaret, the widow of King James IV and mother to James V, who at this time was still in his minority. Margaret had been appointed Regent, but on the marriage taking place Arran mustered his men and marched into Edinburgh claiming the Regency for himself as the nearest male blood relative to the King. Angus gathered his own men together and followed suit; whereupon Arran attempted to close the gates of the city against him, but gave the order too late. It was clearly not long before fighting would break out, as Arran fixed on a plan to arrest his rival and Angus, gaining wind of the plan, began to barricade sections of the city and prepare himself for battle. The fight itself soon raged up and down the High Street, with the inhabitants of the city leaning out of high windows to watch the proceedings. However, Arran had not counted on the enmity of the people of the city who had not forgiven him for siding against them in a fiscal dispute some years earlier, and quickly the Hamilton's were put to rout and nearly eighty of their number killed. Arran's brother, Sir Patrick Hamilton, was cut down in the fight, and the Earl himself only narrowly escaped with his son by fleeing down Blackfriars Wynd, commandeering a packhorse and swimming it across the Nor Loch to safety.

MAY

Calton Hill in the early twentieth century. (Author's Collection)

1 MAY 1728

James Inglis was executed by hanging in the Grassmarket for the crimes of horse stealing and sheep clipping. This was his second conviction for the very same crimes. On the first occasion he had been sentenced to be whipped through the streets and banished from the town.

2 MAY 1928

When 51-year-old Andrew Muir died in his bed on this date, his wife was too ill to summon assistance. It was only two days later, when neighbours noticed the lack of activity and other signs of occupation, that police were notified and gained admission by force, whereby Muir's body was discovered and the now seriously ill Mrs Muir taken to the Royal Infirmary.

3 MAY 1682

A riot broke out on the streets of Edinburgh when a group of young men – who had been imprisoned in the city on a trivial charge – were being marched to Leith to be put on a ship bound for Holland to serve in the army of the Prince of Orange. As they passed along the road, a woman selling pottery called out to them 'pressed or not pressed?' whereupon one of the young lads shouted back 'pressed!' At this the woman started throwing shards of broken pottery at the soldiers escorting the lads, and others joined in, obtaining ammunition from a site where a new building was under construction. Soon there was a great crowd and the escort was under strenuous attack. Under instruction from their commanding officer, Major Keith, the soldiers turned and fired their weapons into the crowd. In total, seven men and two women were killed in the fusillade, including one pregnant woman who, to spare the immortal soul of the infant, had her belly immediately cut open and the child retrieved and baptised on the spot. Twenty-five more were severely wounded. Three of the rioters were seized and put on trial for incitement, but the assizes found them not guilty and they were released.

4 MAY 1544

Henry VIII of England had been thwarted in 1543 in his attempts to put his own son on the throne of Scotland by marrying the 5-year-old Edward to Mary Queen of Scots, who had ascended the throne two years earlier at only six days old. So he resolved instead to invade the nation to the north, and accordingly his troops arrived this day in Leith and sacked the town prior to the march into the capital to lay siege to the castle. Over the course of the next fortnight Henry's army, under the Earl of Hereford, laid waste to the whole area, leaving both Leith and much of Edinburgh in flames.

5 MAY 1753

It was not uncommon among the poorer classes to dispose of a newborn baby that they were unable, through poverty, to cope with. Female children were especially likely to suffer this fate, as they could not be so easily put out to work at an early age. An example is reported on this date in the *Edinburgh Evening Courant*: 'A new-born female child was found in a pool of water, in an old quarry in Bruntsfield Links, wrapped up in a napkin, with its arms broken and several other marks of violence upon its body.'

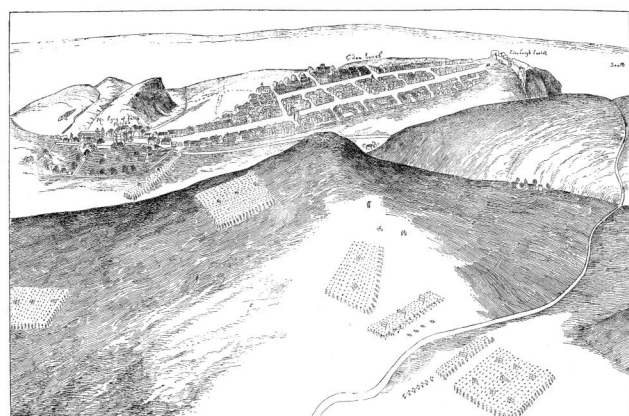

*The Earl of Hereford's army
approaching Edinburgh in 1544.
(Author's Collection)*

6 MAY 1843

The suicide of Thomas Mackay, a gardener from Corstophine, was reported in the *Scotsman* newspaper: 'He was found by the servant maid lying on the floor of his room quite dead, with a discharged pistol in one hand, and a loaded one in the other.' He was said to have been despondent for some time over the loss of some property.

7 MAY 1671

A young woman by the name of Elizabeth Low was found to have a horn growing from her head. At the time it was said to be 11in long and still growing. It was cut from her by a surgeon by the name of Arthur Temple of Ravelrig House. The horn was later kept in the museum of Edinburgh University with a silver plaque describing its origin. Further note of the unfortunate Ms Low states that in 1682 she was still alive, and another horn had begun to grow in the same location.

8 MAY 1691

Although the death of George Mackenzie on this date was an entirely natural one, it is notable for the phenomenon that it sparked which has now become an integral part of the Edinburgh tourist trail. A native of Dundee, Mackenzie became Lord Advocate of Scotland in 1677, and was notorious for his persecution of the Covenenter movement, earning himself the nickname 'Bluidy Mackenzie'. He was a supporter of King James VII and retired his position after James's removal from the throne by William and Mary. He died in Westminster after spending his retirement in Oxford, and his body was brought back to Scotland and interred in Greyfriars Kirkyard. This was the very churchyard where the Covenant, which he so opposed, was originally signed, and many of Mackenzie's victims are buried in the self-same place. Tales of the Mackenzie Poltergeist began around 1998. The story goes that a homeless tramp wandered into the churchyard one night as the gates had been left unlocked. Trying to find shelter, he broke into the Mackenzie mausoleum and, curious as to whether there might be jewels or other treasures around the body, broke open the tomb. Having done so, something happened, although the stories vary between him falling through the floor into a pit of skeletons and the coffin crumbling and showering him in the dust of the corpse. Either way, the man became convinced that a zombie was chasing him, and ran screaming

The haunted Mackenzie Mausoleum in Greyfriars Kirkyard. (Author's Collection)

from the tomb. Since that night there have been over 350 incidents in which people standing close to the Mackenzie tomb have felt themselves pushed or pulled by an unseen hand, have felt unexplained cold or hot areas, or have fainted while being shown around the Black Mauscleum. Almost certainly the Mackenzie Poltergeist is nothing but a tourist phenomenon and the attacks are the result of hysteria in people who have been told to expect something to happen. But there are references in literature dating back to the nineteenth century alluding to the idea that Mackenzie's spirit haunts the mausoleum.

9 MAY 1911

Born in Munich, Sigmund Neuberger became the world's most famous magician and the highest-paid entertainer of his day under the name the Great Lafayette. His signature trick was known as the Lion's Bride, a twenty-five minute act at the climax of which he conjured up a real live lion before the eyes of his stunned audience. At 11 o'clock on this particular night he was approaching the climax of the act at the Empire Theatre in Nicholson Street when a paper lantern used in the staging fell and ignited the scenery. Within minutes the blaze had caught hold and the entire stage area of the theatre was in flames. Initially the audience believed it was part of the act, but as it became apparent the situation was real panic took hold and a general stampede emptied the house within minutes. Lafayette was not so lucky. He had not escaped the blaze and his charred remains were eventually identified among the victims of the fire. In total nine people died, including two hands who were working beneath the stage, a pair of midgets whose remains were initially taken for children, and one of the bandsmen from the theatre.

10 MAY 1926

A platoon of soldiers had a lucky escape when two trains collided outside Portobello on this date, but three other passengers were not so fortunate. The soldiers had travelled in the front carriage of the train, which left Berwick at 1.06 p.m., and had filled the carriage almost to bursting point until they alighted at Portobello, leaving the carriage empty, but for three passengers who joined at that point to travel on to Edinburgh. The collision occurred shortly after, at 3 p.m., as the train entered a tunnel and collided with a goods train, which was in the process of being shunted. The three passengers in the carriage recently vacated by the soldiers were killed, and several in the carriages behind were severely injured.

11 MAY 1929

In front of a crowd of 26,000 people, motorcyclist Walter Brown was killed during the third lap of a four-lap dirt-track race, the first motorsport fatality to occur in Scotland. Brown, from Mussleburgh, was racing in a consolation race at the Marine Gardens Speedway, and was just rounding a bend towards the end of the track when he lost control of his machine and fell to the ground. Another rider, following close behind, was unable to swerve in time to avoid him and his front wheel drove directly into the prone man's back before he also fell – his bike landing on top of the unfortunate Brown. He was quickly extricated and carried from the track, but died a few minutes later from his injuries. Later examination showed that his neck had been dislocated. Brown, who was 32 years of age, had been a prisoner-of-war in the First World War, but had escaped, and had been highly decorated for his bravery in combat.

12 MAY 1933

When John Sullivan was woken by the sound of the one o'clock gun in the Albert Street tenement flat he shared with his parents and sister, he wondered why his mother had allowed him to sleep so long, as he had been intending to go out and look for work that day. As he walked through to the kitchen he was horrified to find both his parents lying dead on the floor in a pool of blood. Their throats had been cut, and investigators later stated that the incident had all the appearances of a double suicide. Sullivan's father had been out of work through illness for some time, but had seemed to be recovering and was intending to return to work. A relapse may have been the reason the couple decided to take such drastic action.

13 MAY 1791

While the City Watch, in the period before a proper police force was formed, were much maligned, it can be argued that theirs was often a difficult and thankless job. The *Edinburgh Herald* of this date reports on one of their number sent to apprehend an artisan wright of the city in consequence of the non-payment of a debt. When asked to accompany him, the wright not only refused, but struck the man with one of his sharp tools with such force that it penetrated his heavy coat and two vests before embedding itself into the flesh of his side, causing such a great loss of blood that he barely survived.

*Captain James Burnet of the City Watch.
(Author's Collection)*

14 MAY 1817

A young woman named Janet Douglas was apprehended this day on a charge of child stealing. Douglas had been laid off as a labourer at a mine in Gilmerton and had been trying to obtain work, but the mine owners were unwilling to employ an unmarried woman in a job that could be worked by a man with a family to support. Starving and desperate, she had kidnapped 5-year-old Margaret Reach from her parents' home in St Cuthbert's, Edinburgh, and had taken her across the Queensferry to Fife and the colliery at Halbeath, where, claiming that she was her own child whom she needed to support, she had found employment. Douglas claimed that it was always her intent to send the child back to her parents as soon as this purpose had been achieved. She was sentenced to death, but the jury recommended her to mercy and the sentence was soon after commuted.

15 MAY 1588

Alison Pearson, strangled and burned for witchcraft on this day in Edinburgh, was a strange one in the litany of women accused of communing with the devil in Scotland. She claimed to have a fairy familiar, which was actually her cousin William Simpson, who at age 8 had been carried off to Egypt by a giant gypsy king. William, she said, came to her in the form of a Green Man and cured her of all ills in return for her faithfulness. He used to appear to her with a band of fairies who would make merry with pipes and dancing and strong drink.

16 MAY 1922

After spending over a month in custody, Duncan Carmichael and David Drummond were charged at Haddington Sheriff Court with the murder of Ellen Blackie, a grocer, in Tranent, East Lothian on 11 April. Mrs Blackie had been found lying on the floor of her shop at around midday on that date. She had been beaten to death with a hammer, which was found lying against a partition next to her. The two men in question had been seen in the village that morning, and were itinerants. They had entered Mrs Blackie's shop at around 8 a.m., purchased some ham, and went next door to ask the woman of the house to fry it for them. After leaving, they were seen on the road out of the village some time later. It appears that nobody was seen entering or leaving the shop in between their purchase and the time the body was found. However, the evidence against them being so slim as to be virtually non-existent, when the case came to court the Solicitor General dismissed all charges and chastised the police for allowing the men to be brought to trial.

17 MAY 1835

When Private James Bell of the 5th Dragoon Guards, stationed at the Piershill Barracks, requested a liberty from evening roll call on this date, the request was denied and he was ordered by Troop Sergeant Major Moorhead to spend the day cleaning the stables. Bell then approached Captain King, asking for the same permission, and King was apparently about to grant this when Moorhead intervened. Bell was said to have been in an agitated state for the rest of the day, and after roll call at seven that evening he was seen to return to his barracks, presumably to collect and load his pistol, whereupon he sought out Moorhead at the No. 13 barracks and shot him. Having done so, he readily gave himself up to other men of the troop, telling them that he had no regrets in shooting a tyrant and that he did it for them as much as himself. Moorhead was mortally wounded, the shot having severed his spine, and died a few days after. Bell was found guilty of murder and executed on 13 July.

18 MAY 1821

David Haggart was brought to Edinburgh in irons on this day after being extradited from Ireland where he had been sentenced to transportation after breaking out of two prisons. Haggart was on the run following the murder of a gaol warden during an escape from a prison in Dumfries. He was tried before the High Court of Justiciary in Edinburgh and sentenced to death. During the month between sentence and execution he wrote a book entitled *The Life of David Haggart, alias John Wilson, alias John Morison, alias Barney McCoul, alias John McColgan, alias Daniel O'Brien, alias the Switcher, written by himself while under sentence of death*. Said to be one of the most fascinating first-hand accounts of the criminal underworld of early nineteenth-century Britain, the book was printed by the Edinburgh publishing house James Ballantyne & Co., and continues to be studied to this day.

19 MAY 1845

Needing to get from Glasgow to Edinburgh as a matter of urgency, a wine merchant by the name of Cooley hired a special train a little before six o'clock in the evening. Unfortunately, the train suffered engine problems and was seriously delayed. It was therefore still on the tracks about a mile and a half outside Edinburgh when the scheduled Glasgow train, which had set off at seven thirty, approached from the rear. The special train had not been fitted with lamps due to the intention that it would arrive during daylight hours, and with the sun having set an hour earlier, the driver of the passenger train failed to notice that the line was occupied and collided with the rear of the train. Mr Cooley, who was seated in one of the rear compartments of the train, was crushed to death in the wreckage. Fortunately, nobody on the scheduled passenger train was seriously injured.

20 MAY: Medieval Edinburgh

In the days before plumbing and sewers, sanitation in the Edinburgh closes consisted of little more than a bucket in a quiet corner. The bucket would then be emptied once or twice a day out of the window and into the close below. The custom was to shout the word 'gardyloo' to warn those who might be passing of the impending event. Gardyloo was a corruption of the French phrase '*garde de l'eau*', or 'watch out for water'. It was then the responsibility of anyone underneath to shout 'haud yer hand', in double quick time or else they were assailed by a very unpleasant shower of rain. It was for this reason that the prices of property decreased the further down the close one travelled. By the bottom, these narrow passages were often little better than running sewers, and the lowest storeys of the buildings were fit only for stabling of animals. On the north side, the raw sewage would spill into the Nor Loch, which at times was essentially a large open cesspit. Edinburgh earned its nickname of Auld Reekie from the pall of smoke that hung perpetually above the city, but it might just as easily have been because of the stench of human waste that penetrated every street.

21 MAY 1650

James Graham, the 1st Marquis of Montrose, was one of the most loyal subjects of King Charles I. After Charles' execution he swore similarly to support his son. Cromwell having taken power in England, the Scots government elected to appoint Charles II as their monarch, but only on condition that he swore to the covenant of true Presbyterianism. When talks broke down between the Scottish nobility and Charles in May 1649, the exiled monarch persuaded Montrose to try to coerce a treaty through an invasion of the country. Montrose

Medieval tenement buildings.
(Author's Collection)

raised a force of Danish and German mercenaries who occupied first the Orkney Islands and from there continued to the mainland. Although after reopening negotiations Charles ordered Montrose to surrender, the news never reached him, and his army was defeated at the Battle of Carbisdale in April 1650. Already under sentence of death from having opposed the covenant in 1645, he was hanged on this day from a gibbet 30ft high at the Mercat Cross. Following execution his body was cut to pieces, the head being displayed on the Tollbooth, the remainder being sent for exhibition in Glasgow, Perth, Sterling and Aberdeen. Finally the body was returned to Edinburgh where it was buried on the Burgh Muir. After the restoration, Charles ordered that this most loyal of his subjects be dug up and afforded a funeral with all the trappings befitting of his status.

22 MAY 1828: The West Port Murders

Burke and Hare continued their killing spree through the summer of 1828. Although the dates are not known for all of their murders, Burke's confession contains some details of the victims, and Hare's confession, though it no longer exists, is said to have, in the main, corroborated Burke's words. The first was a nameless, destitute old woman who came looking for a night's lodging. Next came a woman named Mary Haldane, the mother of two daughters, one of whom had been transported for fourteen years. She fell asleep on straw in Hare's stable and was suffocated there. Her second daughter, Peggy, came looking for her mother and was despatched in the same way. A cinder gatherer named Effie, who often sold pieces of leather to Burke for his work as a cobbler, was another victim. Then came a confused, drunk old woman, who was being led through the West Port by a policeman, whom Burke relieved of his burden by saying he would help her home. An elderly grandmother and her 12-year-old grandson were enticed back to the lodgings after she asked Burke for directions. Initially only she was relieved of her life, but then, wondering what to do with the boy, they decided to kill two birds with one stone so to speak. Together their bodies were too large for the usual tea chest and had to be delivered to Surgeon's Square in an old herring barrel.

23 MAY 1730

Private Randal of Cadogan's Regiment, stationed in Leith and being very drunk, discharged his musket into his corporal's breast, who died of the wound the following morning. The soldier was committed to the Canongate Tollbooth on a charge of murder. Found guilty at court, he was sentenced to be hanged on 12 August.

24 MAY 1823

The *Scotsman* newspaper tells the story of an incident which occurred at four o'clock on this morning. A blacksmith in the West Port, having argued with his wife, had decided to leave her and return to his native Glasgow. However, as he passed through the streets with his bundle under his arm, a watchman, thinking he might be up to no good, apprehended him and requested he accompany him to the watch house. Along the way the blacksmith requested permission to use a public convenience and, being released to do so, withdrew a clasp knife from his clothing and cut his own throat, before throwing the knife with some violence at his captor. He was rushed to the Royal Infirmary where it was said his life was despaired of.

25 MAY 1833

In the early hours of this morning, a man by the name of William Hall was apprehended in a lodging house in Bathgate on suspicion of having sexually assaulted and murdered an 8-year-old boy the previous afternoon in nearby Westcraigs. The boy had gone out to herd his father's cow and, when he had not returned at seven o'clock, his mother became worried. Searching the area she found him at ten o'clock that night, naked and lying in a water conduit. He had been strangled, and a knife had been thrust into his rectum deep enough to pierce the bowel. Hall, a tanner of below normal intellect, had been seen near the scene, and was later seen by a girl running away with no shoes on his feet. After his arrest he was lodged in gaol in Linlithgow, where police questioned him with difficulty due to his strong speech defect. Three days later he hung himself in his cell.

26 MAY 1924

William Laurie King, a 22-year-old living with his parents at 2 Wester Coates Terrace, had for years harboured the ambition to become a chemist, despite his father's desire for the lad to follow him into his chartered accountancy firm. William had a small laboratory in an outhouse in the back garden, and here he carried out experiments and perfected his skills to such an extent that later David Peebles, a professional chemist, would say that the boy knew more on the subject than himself. On this date, William had set his mind on an experiment to derive magenta dye from coal tar, and found that he would need a quantity of arsenious oxide. Realising that he needed quite a large quantity, and that he would be unable to obtain this in the normal way, he forged an order from a garage in which he worked part time for the minimum bulk quantity available, 1lb. Four days later, on 30 May, while the family sat down to supper, William's father complained of a burning sensation produced by eating the cheese that his mother had produced. Mother, meanwhile, possibly hurt by the suggestion that her cheese was not of the desired quality, ate a second slice. William ate only a small portion of the cheese, and his brother none at all. Within a few hours, William, his father and his mother were all sick, but brother Alexis was not. By two o'clock the next morning, William's mother lay dead, and a post-mortem revealed that arsenic poisoning had been the cause. William initially did not mention having the arsenic in his possession, and his story of how he came about it was only told after a phial of it was found in his jacket pocket. The phial contained about two ounces. The full packet had been found and confiscated by his mother a few days before her death, and he claimed he later found it on a shelf in the pantry with a corner torn and some of the substance spilled out. His explanations did not convince the police, and he was charged with murder. However, coming to trial that August, what weighed in his favour was that if he had indeed intended to kill either of his parents – and his father was presumed to be the intended victim – then he had been extraordinarily stupid to keep the 'murder weapon' in a place where it would be easily found and traced back to him. He was found not guilty.

27 MAY 1661

Archibald Campbell, 1st Marquess of Argyll, was executed, officially on a charge of treason, but in reality most likely in revenge for the execution of the Marquis of Montrose eleven years earlier. His execution followed closely on the restoration of the monarchy, and might be seen as strange as, ostensibly, he had fought on the Royalist side, had supported the return of Charles II as monarch to Scotland, and had even placed the crown on his head at Scone on 1 January 1651. However, he was also seen as being complicit in Montrose's execution, which he attended, and had been rumoured also to be complicit in the execution of Charles I, on which point he was charged but found not guilty. It had seemed as if he would be released from custody, until a packet of letters to George Monck, 1st Duke of Albemarle, showed that he had collaborated with Cromwell and the Parliamentarians, particularly in putting down a Royalist uprising in Glencairn in 1652. There were many who thought the execution unjust, and many stories arose, such as that on the day of his death, the dogs at his ancestral home took up a strange howling all through the day while staring up at the window of his wife's chamber. Another story tells that during the day prior to his death he was settling affairs with colleagues in his cell when a spirit moved him to tears, and in an attempt to prevent them from seeing this he turned to poke at his fire, whereupon he stated that the Lord spoke to him, saying, 'Son, be of good cheer, your sins are forgiven you.' At the self same moment, a servant

The Maiden, now on display at the National Museum of Scotland. (Author's Collection)

at his home had been in private devotion and had asked God to say exactly these words. On the day of his execution he was transported the short distance from the Tollbooth Gaol to the scaffold surrounded by friends, and was allowed to make a lengthy speech to the assembled masses, after which – and after a short prayer – he submitted himself willingly to the block of 'The Maiden', a Scottish form of the guillotine, and his head was struck from his body. As a sign of respect for his former support of the King his body was not abused, although his head was displayed from the Tollbooth.

28 MAY 1825

The *Scotsman* newspaper reported on this date that 'on Wednesday evening, a decent man was attacked in the Grassmarket by a band of ruffians, among whom was the lad Mackay, who last winter was condemned to be executed for a daring robbery, but was afterwards pardoned owing to a flaw having been discovered in the verdict. The man thus attacked, defended himself, when Mackay stabbed him in the breast with a knife. The wound, if not mortal, was certainly designed to be so; and as it is, it has seriously endangered the man's life.' Alexander Mackay had been sentenced to death on 23 December the previous year for breaking into a watchmaker's shop, having been apprehended red-handed while still in the shop. His reprieve had come through in February after a number of stays of execution. In his initial trial, the newspaper had noted that he had behaved with 'callous indifference' throughout proceedings. He was just 15 years of age.

29 MAY 1917

Joseph Wilmot, a 26-year-old unemployed fitter's labourer, walked into a police station in Glasgow on this day and informed the desk constable that he had murdered his wife and children on the previous Sunday and left their bodies in the tenement flat they shared in Rose Street South Lane, Edinburgh. The police in the capital were quickly informed and forced an

View of the Grassmarket, early 1900s. (Author's Collection)

View over Edinburgh ,with Calton Gaol in the foreground. (S.P. Evans)

entry to the property, where they found Mrs Wilmot and the couple's two young children in exactly the way described. Mrs Wilmot had been first bludgeoned with a hammer and then her throat was cut. The children's throats were also cut. Wilmot stated that he had intended to do away with himself also, by drowning himself in the canal, but that there were too many people around.

30 MAY 1971

A fire which broke out at the Royal British Hotel on Princes' Street on this day claimed the life of a 49-year-old Glasgow woman who became trapped by the flames and was overcome by smoke. Fire investigators soon found evidence that the blaze had been set deliberately, and the finger of suspicion pointed to a young kitchen boy named Robert Docherty who had been employed a few weeks before, since which two other fires had broken out. Docherty initially denied any knowledge, but later admitted setting the first two fires and claimed he had caused the third by accident, throwing a lit cigarette into a full litterbin. However, fire brigade evidence showed that flammable liquids had been used to increase the ferocity of the blaze, and Docherty was found guilty of arson, but acquitted on the charge of culpable homicide.

31 MAY 1878

The Capital Punishment Amendment Act of 1868 ended the practice of public execution. The first hanging in the city following the passing of the Act took place on this day, the subject being Eugène Chantrelle for the murder of his wife on 2 January. In the Calton Gaol, an outhouse had been hastily adapted for the task of becoming the new execution chamber. A hole cut in the floor was covered by a trapdoor, which led to a deep cellar underneath. The trapdoor was held in place by a bolt. The hangman's rope was connected to a hook on a crossbeam between two uprights. The convicted man stood on the trapdoor while the rope was adjusted around his neck, and after the holy man of choice had completed administering to the eternal soul, the bolt was drawn back and the trapdoor opened, allowing for a drop of around 8ft.

JUNE

John Knox's house in the High Street. (Author's Collection)

1 JUNE 1835

Robert Reid of Kirkaldy had a lucky escape in the High Court of Justiciary in Edinburgh on this date, when the case against him for the murder of his wife had to be abandoned. The reason for the abandonment was that the grammatical construction of the charge levelled against him made it unclear as to exactly what crime he was being accused of.

2 JUNE 1581

Being elected Regent during the minority of King James VI seems to have been something of a double-edged sword. Of the four men who carried out the role, the first three died in office in quick succession. James Stewart, 1st Earl of Moray, was assassinated. Matthew Stewart, 4th Earl of Lennox was stabbed to death during a raid in Sterling. John Erskine, 1st Earl of Mar, at least managed to die of natural causes. James Douglas, the 4th Earl of Morton, managed to survive the office, just, resigning on the King's coming of age in 1578, although he still maintained a measure of control over affairs of state. However, in 1581 he was accused of being involved in the murder of Lord Darnley, and was condemned on his own confession that he had previous knowledge of the plot although he denied any direct involvement. He was sentenced to be hung, drawn and quartered, but the sentence was commuted to one of beheading, and was carried out on this date using 'The Maiden'. His head was displayed on a spike at the Tollbooth for eighteen months.

3 JUNE 1817

Being a chimneysweep's boy in the nineteenth century cannot have been an easy life. For 10-year-old James Thompson, this particular day would be worse than most, and his last. His employer, Joseph Rae, had been hired to clean the chimneys in a chapel in Albany Street, and James was sent up the vent to examine what blockages there might be. However, there

James Douglas, 4th Earl of Morton.
(Author's Collection)

was a bend in this particular flue and the boy became stuck fast. Unable to move, Rae began to abuse him, calling him lazy and at one point threatening to buy a barrel of gunpowder and blow both him and the chapel sky high. Witnesses would later state that Rae was in the habit of abusing the boy, frequently striking him, beating him naked with a knotted rope and half starving him. Eventually another sweep, Robert Reid, was brought in, and sent his boy up the flue with a rope to attach to James's legs, and the two men attempted to pull him down using force – using an iron bar as a lever. All this time Thompson had been crying out and begging the men to stop, but eventually he fell silent. By the time the boy was brought out he was dead, caused either by his neck being broken by the force of the pulling, or else by strangulation; his clothes having become rucked up around his neck. Rae and Reid were both charged with murder, but found guilty of culpable homicide, with Rae being transported for fourteen years and Reid for seven.

4 JUNE 1792

On this day, the birthday of King George III, riots broke out across Edinburgh relating to the refusal of Parliament to address the issue of reform of Royal Burghs. Strong protests had been planned well in advance, but were aggravated by the reinforcement of usual street patrols by cavalry troops. The worst of the rioting took place in George Square, outside the house of the Lord's Advocate, Robert Dundas, where an effigy of him was about to be burned when the crowd were attacked by some of his friends to prevent this insult. Beaten back indoors by the crowds, Dundas's house was then attacked with bricks and stones and many of the windows smashed. The 53rd Regiment were called from the castle and, after a reading of the Riot Act, volleys of gunfire were sent into the crowd, killing at least one and wounding, probably mortally, several others. Rioting continued the next day where a crowd was dispersed by troops from Leith from their attempt to destroy the home of Provost Stirling, who had taken refuge in the castle and in whose place an unfortunate doctor by the name of Alexander Wood was almost thrown off the North Bridge before the mistake was discovered.

Looking across George Square. (Author's Collection)

Lord Advocate Robert Dundas (right) with Henry Viscount Melville. (Author's Collection)

5 JUNE 1945

At about nine o'clock on this evening, two young men entered an ice-cream parlour in Portobello High Street with the intention of robbing 82-year-old Guiseppe Demarco and his wife. Police were called and the men ejected from the premises. They returned at ten thirty when Demarco was in the kitchen behind the shop. One of the men held his wife, Maria, to prevent her from intervening, while the other dragged Demarco back into the shop, where he was kicked, strangled and bludgeoned to death with a lemonade bottle. Maria Demarco was also severely beaten. The men, Robert McKenzie Robertson and Timothy Donoghue, then left, taking two bags of money totalling over £100 with them. Robertson was found guilty of culpable homicide, it being taken into account that the deceased man had a pre-existing heart condition that contributed to his death and about which Robertson could not have known. Donoghue was discharged on a verdict of 'not proven', having not taken an active part in the attack.

6 JUNE 1622

On this day a sea battle was fought in Leith harbour. A frigate belonging to King Philip IV of Spain had been lying at anchor for some time while taking on provisions, when two Dutch warships arrived at the same anchorage. When the crews realised the proximity of their enemies – the two countries being at war – they began preparing for battle, and for two hours, muzzle to muzzle, they poured cannon fire onto each other, while hand-to-hand fighting occurred on the decks of all three vessels. An attempt was made by the authorities to end the battle – which was causing great damage to waterside property – by bringing the guns of Edinburgh Castle down to the dockside, but by then the Dutch had forced the badly-damaged Spanish ship out of port, where it was driven onto the rocks, boarded and burned to the keel.

7 JUNE 1898

The death announcements in the *Scotsman* on this date included one George Munro Sym, a 15-year-old Army officer's son from Belgrave Place. Sym had been shot in the face while at school by his close friend Andrew Newlands, who, having found his father's revolver in a drawer, had decided to take it into school to show it around. According to testimony, Newlands had loaded up one of the chambers of the revolver, but believing it to be the fourth chamber, had felt safe to pull the trigger in order to demonstrate the action, and was taken entirely by surprise when the gun went off. He was full of remorse at the killing of his good friend, and the courts accepted that the incident was an accident. The case provided added impetus to the campaign then in progress calling for the licensing of firearms.

8 JUNE 1913

The bodies of two children were found this day lying in water at Niddry Mains Farm, where they had been for at least a year and a half. They were the two sons of Patrick Higgins, an itinerant labourer with previous convictions for child neglect, who had disposed of them when they became too troublesome after his wife's death. Higgins was convicted and sentenced to death. His hanging, at the Calton Gaol on 2 October 1913, was the first to be carried out in Edinburgh during the twentieth century and drew a crowd of some 500 people around the execution chamber.

9 JUNE 1828

When Peter Henderson pleaded guilty at the High Court of Justiciary on this date to abstracting money from five letters before destroying them while engaged in the occupation of a stamper at the Post Office, the judge had to ask him again if he might think about his plea. A guilty verdict, which would be automatic in this case, would bring with it a sentence of hanging, and so essentially Henderson could be said to have been committing suicide. However, his counsel then handed in a letter explaining that they intended, after the verdict, to apply elsewhere for commutation of his sentence on the grounds that Henderson was of below normal intellectual capacity and had not understood the consequences of his actions. The sentence was therefore passed as expected, but a reprieve was obtained less than a month later.

Interior of the High Court of Justiciary. (Author's Collection)

10 JUNE 1717

A thunderstorm broke out on this day of such ferocity that few could remember the like. While it was occurring, a company of men of Jacobite leanings were in a tavern in the Canonmills drinking a toast of health on the birthday of Bonnie Prince Charlie, when a huge clap of thunder caused one to cry out that while men on earth might not be permitted to proclaim their rightful King, God in Heaven had chosen to do so. He may thereafter have regretted his words, for immediately the building was struck by a bolt of lightning, killing two of the party outright and burning another so badly that he died within a few hours.

11 JUNE 1667

The trial of William Douglas, accused of the killing of Sir James Home of Eccles in a duel, resulted in his being sentenced to beheading on this date. The two men, together with two others with whom they had been drinking, had an altercation regarding loyalty to the king. They had exited the tavern and hailed a coach, telling the driver to take them to a remote spot on the shoreline near Leith Links. During the coach ride the four men remained entirely civil, but on arriving at the designated spot, they emerged from the coach and immediately took up arms and set to fighting. During this, a troop of the King's Lifeguard rode up and ordered the men to stop, but they refused to do so. The fighting ended immediately Home was struck down, and the man was carried to a nearby house where it was said that Douglas asked, and was granted, pardon from him before he died.

12 JUNE 1864

At 6 a.m. on this morning the broken body of James Henderson, a soldier in the 92nd Highlander Regiment, was found in West Princes' Street Gardens, at the foot of Castle Rock. It transpired that Henderson had married a few weeks earlier without regimental approval, and that the rules of the regiment meant that his wife was not allowed to live with him in barracks in the castle. It was therefore supposed that he was endeavouring to sneak out of the confines of camp in order to indulge in marital pleasures when he must have missed his footing and plunged to his death.

13 JUNE 1881

Tried before the High Court of Justiciary on this day were sailors David Rintoul and John Henry Shewan, from the ship *Vigilant*, on the charge of having murdered Police Constable George Lowe of the Edinburgh City Police while engaged in a burglary. The two men had forced the door to a common passage within a tenement of houses in Elm Row, intending to rob the premises of two shops which could be accessed from the lowest level of the stairwell. Police Constable Lowe surprised them in the passage and ordered them to accompany him to the police office, whereupon the pair set about him, Rintoul striking him several blows with an iron bar and Shewan stabbing him repeatedly with a dagger. The pair were found guilty of assault and culpable homicide respectively. Rintoul was imprisoned for eighteen months, Shewan for fifteen years.

14 JUNE 1733

A man named Crookbane, a perfumer of gloves, while walking in the Netherbow, was, according to the *Edinburgh Evening Courant*, 'knocked down with a stone, and otherwise beat and abused in so cruel a manner that he died in a few hours.' His brother was also said to have been beaten 'so that his life is despaired of.' A shoemaker by the name of Christie was apprehended for the crime and confessed his guilt. However, he was eventually spared trial on a technicality, his rights having been contravened by the trial not being organised against him in a timely enough manner. The matter was passed on to the High Lords of Justiciary, whose decision was to transport him to America on the condition that should he return he would be imprisoned and whipped at the hands of the common hangman.

15 JUNE 1691

After the accession to the throne of William and Mary, Jacobites loyal to the former King James VII held out in certain parts of Scotland until the Battle of Killiecrankie in 1689. After this, all of Scotland came under the rule of the new monarchs, except for one location, the Bass Rock in the mouth of the Firth of Forth, where a garrison of Jacobite prisoners held out until 1690. The heavily fortified rock had been used as a maximum-security prison for troublesome prisoners, initially Covenanters and later Jacobites, for some years. On this date, the men took control of the rock a second time. During a time when the governor was absent, and most of the guards were outside the prison taking a delivery of coal, four of the prisoners closed the gates against them and set up a defence of their new realm. There they remained for the next three years, the only part of the British realm still claiming James's sovereignty, in defiance of anything that William's army could throw against them, and with support from elements of the French navy and from Jacobite supporters on the mainland. One attempt to draw them out occurred in 1693, when a man named Trotter who had been running supplies of provisions to them was sentenced to death for treason. The decision was taken to carry out the execution at Castleton because it was within sight of the fortifications on the island. However, the men who occupied the island, now sixteen in number, fired their guns at the mainland to disperse the crowd and the proceedings had to be moved elsewhere.

The occupation ended on 20 April 1694. Nearing the end of their provisions and facing starvation, the men invited peace envoys to open negotiations with them, and, having specially kept back a supply of luxury goods, treated them to an impressive banquet, giving the impression that they were well-stocked for many years to come. The ruse worked and, in order to end the occupation quickly, they were allowed to leave the rock with their lives, their liberty, and no confiscation of property.

The Bass Rock from Tantallon Castle. (Andrew McMillan)

16 JUNE 1938

While using a gas iron on this date, 71-year-old Bessie Wyllie of Stockbridge collapsed and, pulling the iron on top of herself, set her own clothing on fire. Although help arrived within minutes, by the time she was rescued her burns were too severe and she died shortly afterwards.

17 JUNE 1605

Fighting broke out on the High Street by the Salt Tron between the sons of the Lairds of Edzell and Pitarrow, both of whom were committed to prison for failing to contain their offspring. The fight lasted two hours, and a man named Guthrie, one of the Pitarrow party described as a 'very pretty young man', was killed. Foreseeing difficulties, Edzell had a surgeon examine the corpse and pronounce that the young man had not been killed in the fighting but had been crushed in the throng of bodies.

18 JUNE 1919

When 23-year-old Mona Dunn fell for the charms of South African medical student John Moir Du Toit, she believed that her feelings were reciprocated. But when she fell pregnant by the young man, he made it clear that, despite her affection, he wanted no more to do with her. Eventually he agreed to help her find someone who could 'take care of her problem', but was unwilling to help financially or otherwise. Dunn eventually went with a friend, Gladys Wolhuter, to the home of a Mrs Nan Main, where the illegal backstreet abortion was carried out on this date. By midnight Mona was dead, the medical verdict being excessive bleeding from a rupture of the womb. Nan Main was tried and found guilty of culpable homicide, and was sent to prison for five years.

19 JUNE 1820

James Maccoul, or Moffat, who was sentenced to death on this date at the High Court of Justiciary, was said to be a villain of uncommon intelligence and enterprise. He was convicted of having robbed a bank in Glasgow eight years earlier, a crime he had been suspected of for all that time but where evidence had not been present to pin the deed on him. He had finally been caught changing some of the ill-gotten money from the raid in Leith, and this had been confiscated by the State. From that time, Maccoul set about a series of litigations in an attempt to retrieve the money, and it was one of these court cases which finally turned up the evidence to convict him of the original crime. Justice, however, was to be cheated once again. By the time of his conviction Maccoul was already mortally ill, and was said to have spent his time in the Calton Gaol in paroxysms of agony before dying a week or so before his appointed date of execution.

20 JUNE 1936

Tragedy struck at the Royal Forth Yacht Club regatta off the coast of Granton. During the last race of the day, five yachts were sailing the course when a heavy squall hit. The crew of the *Daydream* were tacking towards Leith and saw the yacht *Jabberwock* cross over their stern tacking for the north shore. At that point the squall struck and carried away their main stay, and when they put about on the other tack it carried away their jib also. Struggling to repair the damage, they noticed that the other yacht was gone, and assumed she had made for shore to escape the weather. However, when they returned to port themselves it was discovered that the *Jabberwock* had not come back. A search was mounted and the yacht was discovered sunk in two-and-a-half fathoms of water, the peak of her sail just breaking the surface of the water. None of the four-man crew survived.

21 JUNE 1864

The last public execution in Edinburgh took place at the head of Liberton's Wynd on this date. A large crowd gathered to watch the final moments in the life of George Bryce as he paid the ultimate penalty of law for the murder of Jane Seton in the village of Ratho on 16 April. Bryce, a young man employed as a carter by his father, had become enamoured of the cook in the employ of their neighbour, Mr Robert Tod. The pair had become intimate, but Bryce had a reputation for drinking and violent behaviour, and Ms Seton, the nursemaid in the same household, warned her fellow employee of the dangers of continuing the affair. The cook had therefore grown cold towards Bryce, who as a result began to harbour feelings of resentment towards Seton. On the day in question he had, it was said, been drinking for several days, and barged into the Tod household, attacked Ms Seton and began to strangle her. The cook intervened, beating him away with an umbrella, and the young nurse escaped and ran to a neighbour's house. But before she could get there Bryce gave chase, caught her up, and slit her throat with a razor.

22 JUNE 1679

The Battle of Bothwell Bridge was the beginning of one of the more shameful episodes in Edinburgh's history. A 5,000-strong army raised by Lord Linlithgow, under the command of the Duke of Monmouth, one of the most experienced generals in the country, met a Covenanter army, around the same strength, but a disorganised rag-tag bunch who could not agree as to who should be their leaders, on the banks of the Clyde. The battle began at 7 a.m., and by 10 a.m. it was all over, the Covenanters put to rout with around 400 dead and 1,200 captured and taken prisoner. The prisoners were rounded up and marched to Edinburgh, where they were placed in an enclosure in the grounds of the Greyfriars Kirk to await their fate. For the next five months they remained in this area, confined by four walls and barred gates, but with no roof and no protection from the elements. They were given little food or drink and were generally ill abused by their guards. Large numbers died of exposure or starvation, and those that survived were mostly either executed or transported for life to the colonies to live out their days as slaves. The walls of the Covenanters Prison remain to this day and are part of the Edinburgh tourist trail. In 1706 the Martyr's Monument was erected in the kirkyard as a memorial.

Entrance to the Covenanter's Prison, Greyfriars Kirkyard. (Author's Collection)

23 JUNE 1923

Robert Cree, an unmarried railwayman and former soldier, had travelled from his home in Dunfermline into Edinburgh for the football, with the intent of catching the last train home. After the game he got to drinking and fell in with a local prostitute, Catherine Donaghue, known in the district as Katie Rose. After consuming a considerable quantity of alcohol, they retired to Katie's lodging at 4 Jamaica Street. But as they entered they found Philip Murray, Katie's regular partner, dressed and lying on her bed. As soon as they entered the room he jumped up, head-butted Cree and began to demand his money. The fracas that followed resulted in Cree being thrown from the window to his death on the pavement below. At trial Murray was blamed for the incident and sentenced to hanging, but neighbours believed that Donoghue was also involved. It was never established whether she had taken the man home with the intention of transacting her usual business, or whether robbery had been the scheme all along.

24 JUNE 1902

We think of gun rampages as a modern phenomenon, but on this date an earlier example of the crime occurred in Edinburgh. The perpetrator was one Daniel McClinton, a servant at a laboratory in the Surgeon's Hall. The lab was run by two brothers, Stevenson and William Ivison Macadam, both consultant analysts and Fellows of the Chemical Society. On the morning in question Stevenson, William and McClinton were at work in the laboratory, together with two other scientists, James Kirkcaldie and a man named Lyle. William, the older brother, was in his uniform as a Major in the 1st Lothian Volunteer Brigade, as he was due to leave for London that day to attend the coronation of Edward VII. During the morning McClinton left, saying he had some business in town. Instead, he returned to his home, where he collected his rifle, telling his wife he was going to do some volley shooting later, and then went back to his workplace. Re-entering the laboratory carrying the rifle, and with an ammunition bag on his shoulder, he crossed the room quickly, levelled the rifle and fired two rounds at William, who staggered a few steps to the side and then fell to the ground dead. Stevenson, unaware of his brother's condition, approached McClinton, who waved the rifle in his direction. 'Stand where you are!' he ordered. 'I won't shoot you if you stand where you are. If you interfere with me I will, but if you don't, I will not.' At this moment Kirkcaldie tried to make for an exit door, whereupon McClinton turned and fired the rifle at him.

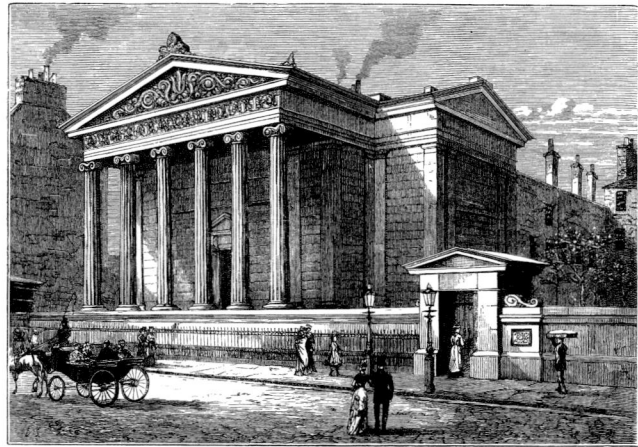

Surgeon's Hall.
(Author's Collection)

The scientist ducked behind a bench and the bullet struck the wall above his head. McClinton then began to prowl around the room while Stevenson tried to persuade him to give up his gun. At this point a telephone rang and Stevenson, saying he would need to answer it, made for the door – which suddenly opened and a student named Forbes stepped inside. Forbes was shot twice and fell on his back just inside the door. He died later in hospital. Stevenson again tried to reason with McClinton, who told him he had two more that he wanted to get level with. But then, in a moment of apparent clarity, he finally opened the breech of the rifle and emptied the remaining cartridges on the floor before handing over the weapon. At trial his defence pleaded insanity, but this was rejected as McClinton appeared to have been entirely lucid throughout his rampage. He was found guilty of culpable homicide and sentenced to life imprisonment, although the verdict was arrived at by a majority of 8–7, the remainder opting for the charge of murder which would have carried the sentence of death.

25 JUNE 1591

Travelling to Denmark with the intention of bringing his bride, the princess of that country, back to Scotland, King James VI was detained on the journey by a storm, which blew up and nearly wrecked his ship. The following year, a young woman by the name of Gellie Duncan was denounced by neighbours as a witch and, under torture, confessed to being in league with the devil and gave up the names of several others with whom she had conspired. These were soon arrested and another of their number, Agnes Sampson, also under torture, confessed that the group had conjured the storm deliberately in an attempt on the life of the King, claiming that Satan had compelled them to do so by declaring that James was the greatest enemy he had ever had. The group were all sentenced to the usual fate of witches at the time of being strangled and their bodies burned. However, one of their number, Euphemia Macalzean, was considered particularly infamous and was said to have poisoned those who had stood in her way, and was therefore thought deserving of much harsher treatment. Macalzean was executed on this date, sentenced to be 'bound to a stake and burned in ashes, quick [alive] to the death,' notwithstanding that she was a noblewoman, the daughter of Lord Cliftonhall. The sentence, considered the harshest that could be handed down on those accused of witchcraft, was carried out in the presence of King James himself.

King James VI of Scotland.
(Author's Collection)

26 JUNE 1604

Robert Weir, the murderer of John Kincaid of Warriston, captured after four years on the run, was executed for his crime by being broken on the wheel. This form of execution was rarely used in Scotland, being among the most barbaric in medieval times. The victim was stretched across a cartwheel, his limbs running along the spokes, whereupon the executioner, with a heavy mallet, would break those limbs in several places. The broken limbs would then be wrapped around the wheel spokes, and the whole raised onto a tall pole where the man would be left to die from dehydration or shock, while birds pecked at his still living body.

27 JUNE 1791

A childish quarrel on this date led to brutal murder. The daughters of Mary Frazer and John Saxton, who lived one above the other in the same house in the West Port, were arguing in the street when Frazer called her child to her and asked what the quarrel concerned. 'She called my father a beggar-man,' she was told, whereupon Frazer replied, 'You might have called her the pig-wife's daughter.' On hearing this insult, Saxton came rushing down the stairs with his three sisters, and all four set to beating the woman with sticks. Frazer lingered for a week before succumbing to her injuries the following Sunday.

28 JUNE 1685

Sentencing in the Middle Ages was often very specific. An example of this involves Richard Rumbold, an English soldier, who was punished for taking part in a plot under the Earl of Argyll to usurp the throne from King James VII. The sentence read as follows: 'Rumbold to be immediately taken from the bar in the lay town council house to be examined by the magistrates and hear prayer in the ordinary way, and that the order may be given by them to the said magistrates that a scaffold and a high gibbet be erected above the cross towards the West, and that after he is examined and prayer heard, they cause him to be led down by the hangman, having his hat on to the scaffold, and there to be hoisted up the gibbet with a rope about his neck, and immediately to be let down and the rope being about his neck, his heart to be cut out by the hangman and shown to the people upon the point of a bayonet or dagger, round about on the scaffold, who is to express these words, "Here is the heart of a bloody traitor and murderer"; and which thereafter the hangman is with disdain to cast in a fire prepared of purpose on the scaffold; and thereafter his head to be cut off and shown to the people by the hangman in manner foresaid and expressing the former words; and then his body to be quartered, and one part thereof to be affixed at the Port or Tollbooth of Glasgow, another at Jedburgh, a third at Dumfries, and a fourth at the New Town of Galloway; his head to be affixed at the West Port of Edinburgh on a high pole.'

29 JUNE 1902

Helen Black was said to have been a clean-living woman of sober habits until she took up with Hugh Mooney. Thereafter, for the next three years, hers was a life of itinerancy and drunkenness, living from hand-to-mouth in cheap lodgings on the Cowgate and spending what little the couple had on drink. This state lasted until, in a drunken rage, Mooney beat the woman to death with his own wooden leg in their tenement room. The fracas was heard going on throughout the night by neighbours, Helen frequently crying out the words 'Murder!', and 'Is everybody dead?' But nobody was brave enough to go to her aid, and when one neighbour sent a child to look for a constable, Mooney burst into her room and threatened her as well. He was sentenced to spend the rest of his life behind bars.

30 JUNE 1934

At some time just before midnight on this date, a young man named Giovanni Belmonte was assaulted and left unconscious on the North Bridge. Being found by passers-by, he was carried to a police box in Hunter Square, and from there to the Royal Infirmary where he died from his injuries ten days later. John McHugh was arrested and charged with the assault, but on appearance in court on 14 July the charge was reduced to one of culpable homicide.

JULY

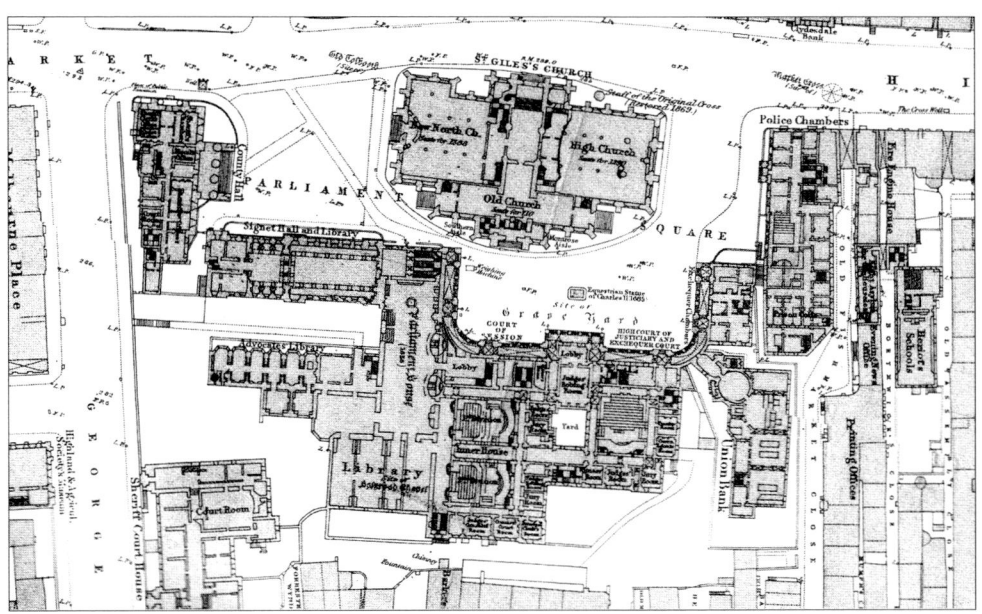

Map of Parliament Square, 1856, showing St Giles' Cathedral, and the locations of the Mercat Cross, the High Court of Justiciary, and the site of public executions (top left-hand corner of County Hall). (Author's Collection)

1 JULY 1600

The custom of marrying for political or familial alliance at this time in history most likely created quite a few unhappy marriages. Young Jean Livingston was 15 years of age when she became Lady Warriston through marriage to the similarly young John Kincaid. Their life together does not seem to have been in any way pleasant, and after six years of marriage and with an infant child, the last straw for her appears to have been an argument over the dinner table in which he struck her several times and sank his teeth into her arm. Informing her faithful nursemaid, Janet Murdo, who had been with her since childhood, that she wished her husband dead, the older woman agreed to procure a person who would perform the deed, or else to carry it out herself. She found a young stable boy named Robert Weir from Holyrood, who sneaked into Kincaid's bedroom on this night, accompanied by Lady Warriston. When Kincaid awoke the two struggled, and Weir first struck him on the jugular vein and then strangled him to death. The crime being quickly discovered, Weir fled the city while Lady Warriston, the nursemaid and two other women were taken into custody. The trial took place two days later on 3 July, when it is believed that one of the other two accomplices may have turned Kings Evidence to procure the conviction. Lady Warriston was beheaded by The Maiden at the Canongate on 5 July, just four days after the crime was committed, while the nursemaid and one of the other two women were burned at the stake in the Grassmarket on the same day.

2 JULY: Medieval Edinburgh

In the years before forensic science, a successful conviction generally relied on either witness testimony or, if no witnesses were to be found, the confession of the accused. When a suspect would not confess, the judiciary had the option of ordering torture. One thing that seems unique to Scotland is the cute names given to torture devices. Alongside the usual methods of sleep deprivation, burning and pulling nails and teeth with pincers, two of the most popular methods were the 'bootikins' and the 'thumbikins'. The thumbikins was essentially a thumbscrew. It consisted of a U-shaped metal bar with a second metal plate inside attached with a screw device, the thumbs were inserted and the screw tightened until the bones of the thumbs began to break. This would cause excruciating pain not only in the thumbs themselves, but up the arms and across the back. The bootikins was similarly a crushing device. It consisted of semi-circular wooden plates attached to the front and back of the leg between the ankle and knee, wooden wedges would then be driven into the gaps, which would crush the bones until they splintered, often crushing all the way down to the marrow. A person tortured with the Bootikins would generally be crippled for life, albeit that once in that position their life was not likely to last much longer anyway.

3 JULY 1702

An explosion on this day wrecked much of the town of Leith. Unfortunately very little of this event has been recorded, but a petition to the Privy Council from the inhabitants of the town seeking compensation provides some detail. 'It pleased the great and holy God to visit this town, for their heinous sins against him, with a very terrible and sudden stroke, which was occasioned by the firing of thirty-three barrels of powder; which dreadful blast, as it was heard even at many miles distance with great tenor and amazement, so it hath caused great ruin and desolation in this place. It smote seven or eight persons at least with sudden death, and turned the houses next adjacent to ruinous heaps, teared off the roof, beat out the windows, and broke out the timber partitions of a great many houses and biggings even to a great distance. Few houses in the town did escape some damage, and all this in a moment

Medieval instruments of torture on display in the National Museum of Scotland, including the branks and the thumbikins. (Author's Collection)

of time; so that the merciful conduct of Divine Providence hath been very admirable in the preservation of hundreds of people, whose lives were exposed to manifold sudden dangers, seeing they had not so much previous warning as to shift a foot for their own preservation, much less to remove their plenishing.'

4 JULY 1828: The West Port Murders

Sometime in early July Burke and Hare had a falling out and Burke and his wife moved out of Hare's lodging house into a home of their own a few streets away. Burke and Helen had left Edinburgh for a visit to Falkirk on 24 June, and the argument may have begun before then. Helen was a quarrelsome woman and their fighting had become more and more of a problem, so much so that Maggie Hare had suggested she become the next 'merchandise'. A plan was hatched that Burke should leave while Hare did the business, and that Burke should then send a letter from Falkirk saying that Helen had died and been buried there, so as to assuage suspicion from the neighbours. However, Burke refused to go along with this. The dispute may also have been because Burke discovered on his return that Hare had done some business with Dr Knox and his assistants and had not cut his partner in on the spoils. Shortly after this split, Ann McDougal, a cousin of Helen's ex-husband, came to visit; a big mistake on her part. The former partners put their differences aside and Ann was soon lying on Knox's slab.

5 JULY 1607

Following the slaughter of his uncle, Sir Walter Lyndsay by David, Master of Crawford, on his estates in Forfarshire, the young Laird of Edzell swore vengeance. On this evening, while

*Helen McDougal, common-law wife
of William Burke, contemporary
trial portrait. (S.P. Evans)*

passing up the High Street in the company of Alexander, Lord Spynie and Sir James Douglas of Drumlanrig, Crawford was set upon by Edzell and eight compatriots. All three men were severely wounded, and Spynie died as a result eleven days later. Edzell fled, distraught at having caused the death of Spynie, another uncle whom he had always regarded with affection, and who had been working towards effecting reconciliation between Edzell and Crawford.

6 JULY 1899

Frederick Warwick, a telegraph superintendent in Malta, had been suffering an illness and was advised to return to Britain for rest. Taking rooms in Bruntsfield Place, he moved into the lodging with his wife, two sons aged 11 and 9 and a daughter a year or two younger. At about half past four in the morning on this date their landlady was woken by a gunshot followed by a loud scream. Crossing the passage, she found Mrs Warwick crying out that her husband was dead. A doctor who lived across the road was called and, entering the room, found Mr Warwick had taken his own life with a bullet through his right temple. On the floor lay a revolver from which three bullets had been fired. The other two shots had been intended to kill his two sons, but the shot fired at the older boy, Arthur, had missed entirely. Younger son Frederick, on the other hand, had been hit in the head and, though still breathing, died before he could be transported to a hospital. No explanation for the incident was ever forthcoming, although a pair of telegrams written by Warwick suggested that he had planned the shooting in advance.

7 JULY 1830

Reported in the *Scotsman* of this date: '... as a servant of Mr Carse, the stagecoach proprietor, Leith Walk, was leading out in a colt-halter, a horse with a hay cart attached to fetch home a load of cut grass, the animal, unaccustomed to be without his bridle and blinds, got alarmed, and suddenly darted forward; the top frame of the cart striking the driver on the back of the head, knocked him down, when one of the wheels passing obliquely over his body, crushed him so severely that he soon after expired. He has left a widow and five destitute children.'

8 JULY 1682

While riding from Edinburgh to his ancestral home of Drum, James Somerville came across two friends fighting a duel in the road. Dismounting his horse he attempted to come between the two and prevent bloodshed. However, the two men, Thomas Learmouth and Hew Paterson, were both drunk and determined to continue their fight. As he tried to separate them, Somerville was struck by Paterson's blade and as a result died two days later.

9 JULY 1790

Life expectancy being so much shorter in centuries gone by, it was considered noteworthy by the *Edinburgh Herald* to mention the death of Nicholas Coates on this date. He was 97 years of age, and his wife, of similar age, had died just one day before. The pair had been married for between seventy and eighty years.

10 JULY 1824

Terrance DeLancey died from blood poisoning caused by a leg wound after being struck by an officer of the City Watch. DeLancey's wife, Margaret, had gone out on the streets in the early hours of the morning of the 8th in search of her husband, and had been apprehended by a watchman who mistook her for a prostitute. Attempting to take her to the police office, she resisted and he struck her. Seeing this, her husband had tried to wrestle the baton away from the watchman and was immediately set on by the man and two other members of the watch, one of whom struck a blow across his legs which shattered the bone. Protesting that his leg was broken, the man was dragged to the police office and charged, the watchmen insisting all this time that he was feigning the injury. It wasn't until the following day that he was able to receive medical treatment, by which time he was insensible, and the broken bone was not discovered until the post-mortem on the body.

11 JULY 1668

While climbing into the coach in which Archbishop Thomas Sharpe of St Andrews was waiting in the High Street, the Bishop of Orkney was seriously injured when a man stepped out from behind the coach and fired a pistol at him, breaking his left arm above the wrist with five balls of shot. The assailant was a preacher by the name of James Mitchell, and his intended target had been the Archbishop whom he accused of being weak in the cause of Presbyterianism. Following the shooting Mitchell ran off down the High Street to Niddry's Wynd, where a man stepped out to apprehend him, upon which Mitchell drew a second pistol and was allowed to pass. Entering a house in Steven Law's Close, he changed his clothes and passed back onto the street unhindered and unnoticed. His eventual arrest for the crime did not come until six years later, when he was spotted and recognised by Archbishop Sharpe himself. Mitchell would spend several years in prison before eventually being executed. Sharpe himself, however, did not entirely escape the fate his assailant had intended for him. He was brutally murdered eleven years later near St Andrews by a group of Covenanters who had suffered for their religious leanings.

12 JULY 1945

The death of a child is always a tragedy, but more so when that death occurs in gruesome circumstances. On this day, 8-year-old Phyllis Merritt was found in an air-raid shelter between St John's Hill and Holyrood Road, close to where the Parliament building now stands. She had been assaulted, strangled, her head battered against the wall, and then dragged to the ground where she had been struck on the head repeatedly with rocks until she was dead. Suspicion fell on her 17-year-old uncle, Robert Rigg, who discovered the body, and this suspicion seemed to be confirmed when the investigating officer, Superintendent William Merrilees, testified that Rigg had confessed to him under caution. However, as no statement had been written and formally signed, the judge presiding over Rigg's case refused to admit the evidence, as a result of which Rigg was found not guilty.

13 JULY 1902

When Sir Henry Littlejohn, the police surgeon for Edinburgh, was called to a tenement flat at Potterow in the early hours of this morning, he found a woman named Mary Hastie lying in the bed of her neighbours, the Adamsons, with such severe injuries to her face and head as to make her almost unrecognisable as a human being. Mrs Hastie died around two hours later from concussion, haemorrhage and a combination of other injuries. It transpired that while her husband and son had been out for the evening, she had been drinking with Mrs Adamson and another neighbour, Mrs Marion Fellowes, when John Adamson had returned home. Finding his wife the worse for drink, he had blamed Mrs Hastie for giving her the drink and began to strike her before dragging her into his own home and continuing the attack during which he used several heavy implements upon her. He was sentenced to twenty years in prison.

14 JULY 1819

'Hamesucken' was an offence peculiar to the Scottish statute books, and essentially consisted of housebreaking with an element of violence. James Whiteford was tried at the High Court of Justiciary for hamesucken on this date. The incident occurred at 3 a.m. on 27 March, when Henry Duncan, a publican of Hopetoun Wood, was woken from his sleep by someone banging on his door and requesting a bottle of porter. Refusing to come down to let the man in at that hour, a moment or two later the shutter of his window was smashed in, and on his sister opening the door to see what was happening, she was immediately bludgeoned and knocked unconscious. Her assailant, Whiteford, then entered the house and levelled a pistol at Duncan, ordering him to give him all the money he had. He absconded with around £10 in notes and 20s in silver, as well as a bottle of whisky and a loaf of bread. Found guilty, he was sentenced to death and executed on 18 August.

15 JULY 1664

The Earl of Leven, after a lengthy and raucous drinking session with the Earl of Dundee, was crossing to Fife from Edinburgh on the Queensferry when the pair took to a competition to see who could drink the most seawater. On landing, both took dreadfully sick, and Leven died in a fever a few days later.

16 JULY 1946

Mrs Agnes Paton was found dead on this day near the boathouse of St Margaret's Loch, one of the bodies of water surrounding Arthur's Seat. She had been strangled with a necktie by a former soldier named John Rutherford, apparently as part of a pact made by the two some weeks earlier. Mrs Paton, who had regularly been in police cells for drunken behaviour, had several times previously been witnessed playacting being strangled. Rutherford was found guilty of culpable homicide and sentenced to seven years in prison.

17 JULY 1537

Lady Jane Douglas, the wife of Lord Glamis, was renowned as the most beautiful woman in all Scotland. A writer in the *Miscellania Scotia* referred to 'her eyes full, her face oval, her complexion delicate and extremely fair; heaven designed that her mind should want none of those perfections a mortal creature can be capable of; her modesty was admirable, her courage above what could be expected of her sex, her judgement solid, and her carriage winning and affable to her inferiors.' On the death of her husband, her hand was considered a fine prize, and a man named William Lyon hotly pursued his claim, but she preferred another, Alexander Campbell of Skipness, and on their marriage Lyon vowed that he would exact his revenge. Accordingly he accused Lady Jane of an attempt on the life of the King by poison and witchcraft. These being days of high superstition, the charge was taken seriously and Lady Jane, her husband and others implicated in the plot were tortured dreadfully until, to end their suffering, they confessed to the crime. On this date Lady Jane, convicted by her own lips, was led out onto the castle esplanade, and there chained to a stake and burned to ashes in the sight of her husband and young son. The following night Campbell attempted to escape, but fell from the Castle Hill and was found the next morning, his brains dashed out on the rocks. A third man, who was said to have prepared the poison for the conspiracy, was allowed to live, but had his ears severed as punishment.

18 JULY 1715

An indication of the vagueries of Scottish justice involves yet another violent collision on Edinburgh's High Street. In this case the participants were a Mr James Houston and Sir John Shaw, both from Renfrewshire, and two men who had had previous dealings with each other. When they met on the street at the Plainstones, near the Mercat Cross, some form of jostling occurred, although it is not clear which party was to blame. Houston reached for his sword while Shaw produced a cane and began to beat him with it. This was knocked from his hand by Houston, who then ran him through twice. Although seeming at first that he would die from his wounds, Houston survived, albeit in a poor state, and the following year took Shaw to court, and the matter was resolved with the sum of £500 changing hands.

19 JULY 1644

The execution of Sir John Gordon of Haddo on this date was notable mainly for the imprisonment which preceded it. A fiercely loyal Royalist, he was condemned for an attempt to seize Aberdeen on behalf of the King during the Civil War. Taken to Edinburgh, he was kept for the month leading up to his death in a tiny chamber over the porch on the north side of St Giles' Cathedral in the most inhuman conditions. The room was thereafter known as Haddo's Hole until it was eventually demolished during improvements to the cathedral in 1829.

Blackfriar's Wynd.
(Author's Collection)

20 JULY 1588

Francis Stewart Hepburn, the 5th Earl of Bothwell, having succeeded his uncle who was implicated in the murder of Lord Darnley, had fallen into dispute with a noted nobleman named Sir William Stuart of Monckton some weeks earlier. On this date the two men met by accident in the High Street, each with a party of men with them, and a fight broke out. Stuart killed one of Bothwell's servants, but lost his own sword in the fight. Seeing him thus unarmed, Bothwell pursued him into Blackfriar's Wynd where, trapping him unarmed against a wall, he 'strake him in at the back and out at the belly, and killed him.' Bothwell received no punishment for the killing and returned to court shortly afterwards.

21 JULY 1561

One of the frequent street riots that have marred Edinburgh's history occurred on this day. The 'Robin Hood Riot' takes its name from a game or festival common in both Scotland

and England at that period, when one man of the town, usually an individual of great character, would be elected Robin Hood, and all would gather in a field where games and archery would take place while 'Robin' and his cohorts, such as the Abbot of Unreason and the Lord of Inobedience, would lead frolics and play tricks on the authority figures of the town. However, after the Reformation the practice became frowned on, and was eventually outlawed by an Act of Parliament. But the townspeople would not have their fun spoiled, and during May of this year they elected a man named George Dunne for the role, who led the people up and down the High Street causing some havoc. One of their number, James Gillon, was captured by the magistrates, and as an example to prevent such occurrences happening again, he was condemned to be hanged. When the gibbet was erected on this day for the execution to take place, the craftsmen of the town suddenly rushed onto the streets, clad in armour and carrying all manner of weaponry, and seized the town Provost and two Baillies before breaking up the gibbet and beating down the doors of the Tollhouse Gaol with a sledgehammer to retrieve the prisoner. Carrying him to the Nether Bow Port, they found it closed against them, and as they proceeded back up the hill to find another route of exit from the city one of the magistrates, now taking refuge in the Tollhouse, fired a gun into the crowd, wounding one of the men. From there the riot got out of hand with fighting in all parts of the High Street, until troops arrived from the castle to end the trouble. A compromise was eventually reached that all charges against the condemned man would be dropped, and peace was restored.

22 JULY 1826

The *Scotsman* newspaper of this date reports that '... a man, apparently about 50 years of age, was discovered by two boys in the wood on the eastern boundary of the King's Park, suspended by the neck on a tree. They went up to him, and having found he was quite cold, came in to town and gave information at the police office, to which place he was brought in the afternoon. He is very meanly attired, and the only thing found on his person was an empty tobacco pouch.'

23 JULY 1919

William Lamb was well known as a street musician in Edinburgh. Having lost both arms in a motor accident in his native Inverness, he now made a living playing an accordion with his feet. He had been living for some time at 88 Candlemaker Row with Agnes White, a married woman who had separated from her husband some thirteen years earlier as a result of her drinking. On the night in question, Agnes was seen out in a local pub and was said to be somewhat the worse for drink when she returned home. That night a neighbour, Mrs Jane Brodie, described hearing noises like someone falling and furniture being dragged around emanating from the room the couple shared. The following morning Lamb attended a police station and told them his common-law wife had died during the night. Although he claimed not to know how her death occurred, when doctors arrived to examine the body they were clear that the multiple injuries sustained were entirely consistent with her having been kicked and stamped on with heavy boots. Lamb's boots were examined and found to be heavily stained with blood. Lamb was sentenced to death. A bizarre sequel to the case was that the woman's husband, Andrew Sterling, was arrested two days after the court case when it was found that he had remarried despite not being divorced from Agnes, and was therefore guilty of bigamy.

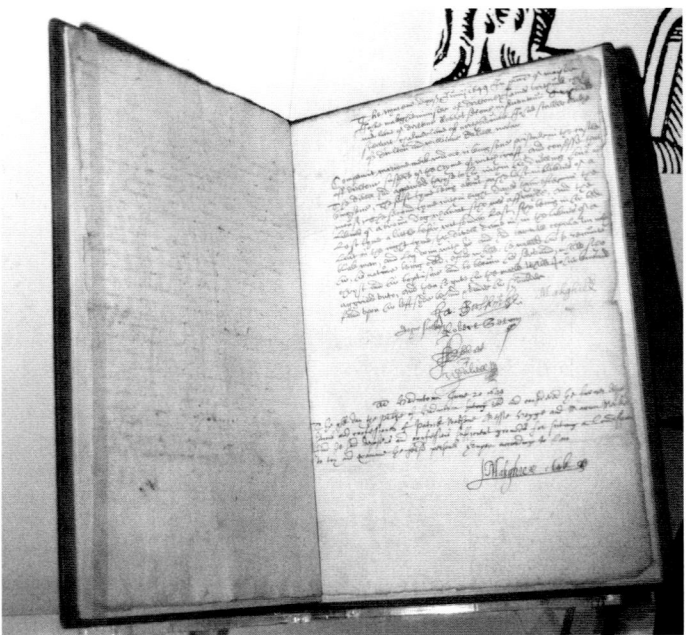

Handwritten confession of witchcraft, obtained by John Kincaid, on display in the National Museum of Scotland. (Author's Collection)

24 JULY 1661

Isobel Johnston of Gullan was indicted for witchcraft on this date. This marked the return to the regular witchcraft prosecutions, which had been suppressed during the interregnum years of Cromwell's rule. With such a great number of trials pending, the next year saw a positive epidemic of them, mostly against men and women whose only real crime was to speak ill of a neighbour shortly before some misfortune had fallen on them. On 23 January 1662, no fewer than thirteen commissions for trial were issued on the charge, this comprising the sole public business of the council that day. Most of the trials hinged on the evidence of confessions made by the accused themselves, although in the majority of cases these confessions had been elicited under extreme torture. One man, by the name of John Kincaid, was employed to test the accused by pricking them with pins to try to find points on their body which elicited no pain, which was said to be a proof of guilt. This continued until April of 1663, when the Privy Council decreed this activity cruel and Kincaid himself was imprisoned. Often, if no sufficient evidence could be found and the cases resulted in an acquittal, the accused would be retained in custody while more evidence was sought against them. Those found guilty were generally submitted to the customary sentence for the crime, that of being burned at the stake.

25 JULY 1894

Around five o'clock on this morning the Harbour Master of the Queen's Dock in Glasgow spotted a body in the water and alerted the river police. Having been pulled from the water and removed to the mortuary, a brick and a heavy piece of coal were found secured to the body of the man, and suicide was presumed. Investigation into his identity revealed that he was one Donald Macdonald, who had been wanted as a murder suspect by the Edinburgh police since the previous Tuesday. On that date the officials of the Royal Insurance Co. in George Street had arrived at the office in the morning to find that their usual arrangements had not been organised for them. Searching for Macdonald in the flat on the premises in which he lived with his sister, the caretaker of the company found the unfortunate woman apparently murdered in her bed. Of Macdonald there was no sign, and he was not seen again until his body was pulled from the water.

26 JULY 1850

When Jane Hamilton, the wife of Irishman William Bennison, passed away in their Leith Walk tenement after a three-day illness, her husband's only reaction was to say, 'Thank God, she has gone to glory, she has gone home.' Jane was Bennison's second wife, a situation complicated by the fact that he had still been married to his first when they had wed. He married Mary Mullen in 1838 in Portadown, but shortly afterwards deserted her and moved to Paisley, where he met and married Jane. Later still he returned to Ireland and Mary, and together they travelled to Airdrie, after which she was never heard of again. He told the court later that she had taken seasick on the voyage from Ireland and had died, and that he had had her buried in a pauper's grave. It seems more likely, however, that she met a similar fate to that of Jane. The undoing of his second wife came after more than ten years of marriage, during which she had borne him a daughter. Bennison, a Methodist, professed to a profound faith, and at his devotions he met another woman, Margaret Robertson, with whom he became enamoured and with whom he was seen going about with at all hours. The pair talked mostly religion, and Miss Robertson would later say she had never been led to believe that he was courting her. William, it seems, had other ideas, and decided that on this occasion it would be better to ensure that his wife was safely out of the way first. Sometime around 12 April he went to a local chemist and bought a tuppence worth of arsenic, claiming it was for the rats. That evening he made a little porridge for his wife, and later she was taken with a violent sickness. She lingered for three days, with many in the neighbourhood coming to visit and help, but only once did a doctor examine her. This was Dr Gillespie, who just happened to be passing. On other occasions, when asked if a doctor had been called, Bennison replied that he had tried but they were busy, and later that it was of no use as his wife was slipping away. Many of the neighbours noted that during this time he went about with a sense of detachment and barely spoke to his wife during her final hours. After her death he arranged a quick funeral, despite her sister asking for a post-mortem examination. When a neighbour's dog that had been fed the remains of the porridge was also found to have died, and with several neighbours voicing their suspicions to the police, Jane's body was exhumed and large quantities of arsenic found in the stomach. In the meantime Bennison had been to the chemist begging them not to tell the authorities about his purchase of the substance. He was found guilty of murder and bigamy on this date, and was executed on 16 August.

27 JULY 1689

The Earl of Balcarres had endured nearly a month in the Tollbooth Gaol, having failed to convince the new government of William and Mary that he did not intend to side with James II in the Jacobite revolution, when on this night he had a visit in his cell from his compatriot, Lord Dundee. He was somewhat surprised to see his old friend draw back the curtain of his bed, look earnestly on him, retire to the fireplace where he stood for a while in a leaning posture, and then leave without saying a word. Balcarras, taken aback, leapt from his bed and called out to his friend to return, but received no answer. At exactly that moment, Lord Dundee was many miles away, breathing his last dying breath on the field at the Battle of Killiecrankie.

28 JULY 1824

Charles McEwan was sentenced on this day to be whipped on his naked back at various places in the city prior to being incarcerated for a year of hard labour in the Bridewell Prison for the crime of biting off the nose of a fellow lodger at a house in Bathgate. The incident had begun with a quarrel between McEwan's wife and that of Hugh Robertson. When Robertson attempted to come between the women, McEwan's wife offered to fight him. Stating that he had never struck a female and did not intend to, the woman then made a push at him whereupon he was said to have tripped her and both fell to the ground. Almost immediately McEwan set about him and, in the course of a struggle, sank his teeth into the man's nose and tore off a portion. A surgeon attempted to re-attach the appendage, but too much time had passed and it would not take.

29 JULY 1924

The Scottish newspapers this morning reported two fatal accidents on the railways occurring on the same day; one in Glasgow and one in Edinburgh. In the Edinburgh incident four women died and thirty more were injured at Haymarket station in a collision between a suburban and a mainline passenger train. The problem seems to have been one of timing. Passengers had just arrived at the station on a special excursion train from St Andrews and, needing to catch the suburban train back to the hostel in which they were staying, the latter had been held up longer than usual while they crossed the bridge to the correct platform. They had just taken their seats when the mainline train to Port Edgar, which had left Waverly four minutes after the suburban train, emerged from the tunnel and ploughed into the back of the train. The accident was blamed on the signal in the tunnel not being set. The Port Edgar train had been slowing at the time, or the accident would likely have been much worse.

30 JULY 1699

If there is one thing the Scots are known for, it is their love of a dram. And if there is one thing than no Scotsman has ever felt any sympathy for, it is the custom of charging duty on their daily tipple. As such, when two agents were dispatched in this month to Prestonpans to verify the suspicion that untaxed liquor would be found in the village, they were unlikely to meet with the co-operation of the locals. Having found and confiscated large quantities of sack and brandy found in the home of a local seaman, they were set upon by the inhabitants of the village, and beaten so badly that one ended up under the care of the surgeon for some considerable time afterwards.

31 JULY 1899

James Begley was sentenced to nine months hard labour in the Sheriff's Court on this date for an assault on his wife that left her disfigured for life and with one eyeball burst, which had to be removed in the Royal Infirmary. Begley pleaded guilty and asked for the Sheriff to take into account that he had never been convicted of assaulting his wife before, and that all of his many previous convictions had been for other offences.

AUGUST

View over Holyrood Palace and Arthur's Seat, early 1900s. (Author's Collection)

1 AUGUST 1623

Thomas Grieve appeared before the Edinburgh Assizes accused of curing people of disease by witchcraft. From a contemporary journalist we learn that he drove their illnesses away by the making of signs and crosses on them, washing their shirts in south-running streams, and the use of anointed cloth and enchanted water. A description of one of his cures stated that he was accused of 'curing James Mudie, his wife and children, of the fever; in curing his wife, by causing ane great fire to be put on, and ane hole to be made in the north side of the house, and ane quick hen to be put furth threat, at three several times, and ta'en in at the house-door witherships; thereafter taking the hen, and putting it under the sick woman's oxter or arm, and therefra carrying it to the fire, where it was halden doun and burnt quick therein.' Found guilty, Grieve was sentenced to be strangled and burned at the stake.

2 AUGUST 1826

A report in this day's *Scotsman* told of a dinner in honour of the poet Robert Fergusson, described by Robert Burns as 'Scotia's Poet', whose life was tragically short and miserable. Born in 1750, by the age of 17 he was supporting his family after his father's death, and although he began to gain some fame as a published poet from 1771 onwards, he suffered severely from depression and mental illness which caused him to stop writing just two years after. While recuperating from this melancholia he had an accident, falling down the stairs and severely damaging his head. After this he was said to be entirely insensible, and died shortly after whilst confined to the Bedlam madhouse.

3 AUGUST 1835

Elizabeth Banks of Dewartown, Midlothian, was executed by hanging on this day for the murder of her husband Peter. The evidence against Banks was entirely circumstantial, but laid a very exact trail. Various witnesses testified that she had been given a shilling in charity and that she spent it on arsenic, which she claimed was required to poison rats. She was then seen mixing a white powder into a drink of salts she prepared for her husband. Shortly thereafter he became ill and started vomiting, whereupon she told neighbours that he had contracted cholera, which at that time had been prevalent, but she called no doctor. After his death, a post-mortem found arsenic in the stomach in lethal quantities. The woman had previously been heard to say that her husband had struck her, and would repent of it. The jury in her trial recommended her to mercy, but when asked on what grounds admitted that they had none, and that it had just been in sympathy.

4 AUGUST 1621

The Five Articles, the basic precepts of the Remonstrant faith devised by the Dutch theologian Jacobus Arminius, were this day accepted into Scottish law, despite the strenuous objections of the Presbyterian faithful. At the moment when the Marquis of Hamilton, commissioner of the Parliament, rose to apply the sceptre to the bills and thus symbolically provide them with royal assent, the greatest thunderstorm in living memory broke over Edinburgh. The sky blackened and the rain fell so heavily that the ceremonial return from Parliament to Holyrood House had to be cancelled as Parliamentarians hurried home in confusion to secure their property. The event was taken by many as a signal of God's displeasure at the new laws, and the day became known as Black Sunday.

The grave of Robert Fergusson, with a headstone erected by Robert Burns. (Author's Collection)

5 AUGUST 1829

A cow feeder and gardener of Ladyfield Place by the name of Crighton was convicted of drunk and disorderly behaviour. The *Edinburgh Evening Courant* tells us he 'knocked down Mr McAra, foreman to a builder, in Moray Place; also knocking down Alexander MacGregor and Andrew Blair, two policemen, and tearing their clothes, while in discharge of their duties.' Crighton was fined four guineas and ordered to pay 10s for repair to the clothes.

6 AUGUST 1938

Jean Powell, a young dairymaid living in Roseburn Place, entered the large house of Ormalie in Corstorphine Road, the residence of Sir William Thomson, in the company of Thompson's gardener James Kirkwall, for what can only be imagined as a sexual adventure in rich surroundings while Sir William was away from home. She did not leave the house alive. Kirkwall, an epileptic who had also suffered from childhood paralysis, killed her with a hammer apparently while under the influence of a fit. He then buried her body in the garden, and invited another man, street cleaner Alexander Watt, into the house to provide him with an alibi. However, his guilt overcoming him, he attended a police station the next morning and confessed the crime. Despite having a history of mental problems, he was adjudged to be sane at the time of the crime and was sent to prison for life.

7 AUGUST 1722

The *Caledonian Mercury* reported on a duel between two soldiers in the Canongate. Captain Chiesley and Lieutenant Moodie, both of the Cameronian Regiment, attacked each other with swords and were both mortally wounded in the conflict. A local private journal gives more detail regarding the incident: 'Having quarrelled some time before in the camp, meeting on the street of the Canongate, the captain, as we are told, asked Mr Moodie whether he had in a certain company called him a coward? And he owning he had, the captain beat him first with his fist, and then with a cane; whereupon Mr Moodie drew his sword, and, shortening it, run the captain into the great artery. The captain, having his sword drawn at the same time, pushed at Mr Moodie, who was rushing on him with his sword shortened, and thus run him into the lower belly, of which in a few minutes he died, without speaking one word, having had no more strength or life left him than to cross the street and reach the foot of the stair of his lodgings, where he dropped down dead. The captain lived only to step into a house nearby, and to pray shortly that God might have mercy on his soul, without speaking a word more. 'Tis said Mr Moodie's lady was looking over the window all the while this bloody tragedy was acting.'

8 AUGUST 1897

Shortly after midnight a private of the Scots Guard, while walking in the Dean Valley on a path alongside the Water of Leith, narrowly escaped injury when something crashed onto the pathway ahead of him. Going to investigate, he found it was the body of an elderly man who had apparently committed suicide by throwing himself from the Dean Bridge, 100ft above. He was found to be 60-year-old William Leyland Parker, a music teacher from Glen Street.

9 AUGUST 1766

On this day both the Earl of Sutherland and his wife were buried in the chapel of Holyrood Palace, having expired within days of each other. Their deaths had been preceded by that of their infant daughter, whose demise the Earl himself accidentally brought about by dropping her while frolicking about. The event had such a devastating effect on his mind that he had withdrawn from society and during this time became afflicted with a fever. His wife, then pregnant once again, ministered to him for twenty-one days before becoming sick from the same cause. Her death preceded his, a fact that was concealed from him until the last, yet with almost his last breath he informed those present that he was going to join her.

10 AUGUST 1831

'The road from Edinburgh to Portobello seems destined at no distant period to become as celebrated as Hounslow Heath or Gad's Hill, unless some active means be resorted to by the public authorities for its security.' So said the *Scotsman* newspaper, illustrating its point by telling that on this date 'a gentleman was attacked between Jock's Lodge and Portobello, by two ferocious ruffians who, after a violent struggle, stabbed him severely, though, we are now glad to say not dangerously. They were providentially scared from their purpose; and information having been immediately given to the police, one of the miscreants was yesterday apprehended.'

Jock's Lodge. (Author's Collection)

11 AUGUST 1927

Having separated from her husband, Mrs Jeanie Ross Paget was said to be in an agitated and disturbed condition while staying with her 8-year-old son Richard at a lodging house at 30 Regent Terrace. Taking him to the bathroom on this night to bathe him before putting him to bed, fellow lodgers noticed that she was a longer time than usual and returned in a more troubled condition than usual. It was later discovered that she had drowned the boy by holding his head under the water. A plea of insanity was accepted and she was detained in a mental institute at Her Majesty's pleasure.

12 AUGUST 1817

On this date, while leaving the city in the direction of Saffindall, the horse pulling the cart of Mr John Tait took fright and overturned its burden, causing severe injury to Mrs Tait and her daughter, and causing their 12-month-old son to be dashed on the ground whereupon he instantly died.

13 AUGUST 1790

A salutary tale appeared in the *Edinburgh Herald* on this date: 'A child of about 2 years old was rode over at Gibb's Entry, Nicolson Street, by a cart loaded with sand, and so much wounded that it died yesterday morning. A precognition has been taken before the Sheriff respecting this melancholy event, and, fortunately for the driver of the cart, it appeared, from the most satisfactory evidence, that he was in no respect to blame; for although driving two carts, he had hold of the halter upon the head of the first horse; that the halter of the horse in the second cart was tied to the first cart; and that he was driving very slow. It further appears that the accident happened by the child's attempting to cross the street betwixt the two carts, and having no person to take charge of it, which ought to be a warning to all parents and others having charge of children not to permit them to stroll on the street unattended.'

14 AUGUST: Working Conditions

When one thinks of slavery in the eighteenth century, it is usually captive Africans working the plantations of the Caribbean or the American Deep South that spring to mind. Few people realise that the workers in the minefields of the Lothian districts around Edinburgh were, to all intents and purposes, slaves also until the late eighteenth century. The actual term used for these workers was 'collier serfs', and the system was known as 'arling'. A miner would be paid a bounty at the commencement of his employment which bound him to the pit owner for life. He could also sell his children to the pit owner and they would, similarly, become his property. The State was also permitted to sell tramps, beggars and those guilty of minor crimes into bondage. Once arled, the men were not allowed to remove themselves from their occupation or seek employment elsewhere. This law was not changed until 1775, when it was allowed that all new men entering the mines should have freedom to change employment if they wished. However, it was not until 1799 that this right was extended to all employees of the mines.

15 AUGUST 1728

A gang appeared at the doorway of the shop belonging to the Dean of Guild Lindsay in Parliament Close a little after eight on this evening, just as the shop boy was closing up.

Some of the gang placed themselves in the entryway to the shop to prevent closure or escape, while others went inside and beat the boy with a hammer until he was dead. They then took a box in which the dues of the Guild were kept.

16 AUGUST 1627

A sea battle having commenced off the Scottish coast between Spanish warships and Dutch fighting ships which were guarding fishing boats, the Dutch fishers had fled to safety and sailed up the Firth of Forth in close formation. Spotted off Leith, the local population, who had been apprised of the sea battle, feared that they were Spaniards headed into port to do mischief. The Privy Council immediately passed a proclamation ordering the men of the city to take up arms and defend the sea shore, while the cannons of Edinburgh Castle were transported as quickly as possible to Leith to join in the defence. The defences remained in place until ten that night when boats sent out from Leith returned to inform the populace that the incursion was a friendly one.

17 AUGUST 1830

Shortly after two o'clock on this afternoon, David Dobie and James Thomson were brought from the prison in preparation for their execution the following morning. Their crime was that they raped, murdered and stole the clothes and money from a Mrs Margaret Paterson. But such were the sexual mores of the day that the trial was held behind closed doors and the newspapers restricted from reporting any but the most basic information. One broadside described how, while travelling with the pair on a cart, 'the two men forced her through a gap in the wall ... into a field, and there, by force, successively violated her person.' It goes on to say that the killing was effected by lacerating her body with one of the bones of her corsets. The judge in the case stated that, 'the utmost stretch of our imagination did not lead us to anticipate the possibility that there were living in the midst of civilized society men who could be guilty

Detail from a broadside on the murder of Margaret Paterson. (Author's Collection)

of still greater atrocities, of more unparalleled brutality, revolting to every feeling that actuates the mind of man. Melancholy it is to think that, had this unprotected female been wandering the world among the most barbarous people, she would have been in a state of comparative safety to what she was within three miles of the metropolis of this most civilized country.'

18 AUGUST 1790

John Cameron had been apprehended by the City Watch for stealing silver spoons on so many occasions that the city assize decided that a more severe punishment than usual should be applied. On this date, Cameron was publicly whipped with sixty lashes on his naked back on the platform at the west end of the Tollbooth Gaol. The desired effect does not seem to have been achieved, however. Two days later, on the Friday, he was apprehended again for the exact same crime. He was sentenced to have the punishment repeated on 1 September. Two days after that was carried out he was arrested again, this time for burglary.

The notorious Tollbooth Gaol. (Author's Collection)

19 AUGUST 1783

The Revd John Mill, a parish minister in Shetland, noted in his diary for this day: 'A globe of fire was seen both at London and Edinburgh, about twenty times larger in appearance than the moon, travelling from the south towards the north-east, and bursting suddenly from a dark cloud, having a tail resembling that of a comet, about an hundred yards from the top of the houses. Its immense size and prodigious brightness terrified the spectators. Next day, 'tis said, a farmer travelling late hours from Edinburgh fell in company with a venerable old man at the back of Salisbury Crags, who had long grey hairs and a staff in his hand. The farmer asked him if he had seen the meteor that flew over Edinburgh? "Alas!" replied he, shaking his head, his eyes sparkling with fire, and a radiance glowing from his countenance. "That ball of fire has passed over more cities and countries than this, and people knew not the danger; and more signs, and strange presages and revolutions would follow, and awful thunders; and earthquakes would swallow up whole islands and cities;" and then, stretching out his hand towards Edinburgh, he said, "None was more ripe for destruction, and that for contempt of gospel light, which would soon be removed, and they would be abandoned to licentiousness and all manner of wickedness. Let the guilty tremble for their destruction draw nigh, but let the chosen watch and pray that they may escape those judgements." He then disappeared with a sharp noise, resembling that of a whip struck in the air.'

20 AUGUST 1618

Thomas Ross, formerly the minister of Cargill in Perthshire, having travelled to Oxford to study, wrote a satire on the character of the Scottish nation, suggesting that the King should exclude all of that nationality from his court, and affixed it to the door of St Mary's Chapel in

View of Arthur's Seat from St Leonards. (Author's Collection)

that city. The King took a dim view of the matter and ordered on this day that he be returned to Edinburgh to stand trial for treasonous libel likely to stir up the people of England to the 'cruel, barbarous, and unmerciful murdering, massacring, and assassine of the haill Scots people, as well noblemen and councillors as others, attendants about his highness's royal person in court.' Claiming temporary insanity, Ross professed penitence and begged the mercy of the court, but received none. He was executed by being hung drawn and quartered, his right hand having first been struck off while alive. His head was displayed on a spike at the Nether Bow and his hand at the West Port.

21 AUGUST 1920

Estranged from his wife, 26-year-old Samuel Fraser called on her at her father's house at 47 St Patrick Square on this evening. Going into the parlour he asked to see their 3-month-old son, who was promptly brought to him. However, when he asked to be left alone with the infant his request was refused, whereupon he went to the window, opened it and threw the child out before climbing through himself and leaping the three storeys to the street below. The baby was killed instantly, and Fraser died a few hours later from head injuries.

22 AUGUST 1821

John Rennie and William Sutherland were executed on this date having been found guilty of three counts of housebreaking and being 'by habit and repute thieves.' Their trial had been turned into something of a farce. They were charged with burglaries at the houses of Mrs Pattison of Leith Links, Mrs Ferrier of Portobello and Mrs Paterson of Canaan. At trial

107

they pleaded guilty to the second of the three, but not guilty to the others, or to the habit and repute. Being told that the death sentence would be passed on them anyway, they then pleaded guilty to all charges, then reconsidered and pleaded not guilty. An accomplice in the robbery at Mrs Ferrier's then testified, after which Rennie decided to plead guilty to all charges again, and Sutherland to the second and third robberies.

23 AUGUST 1950

While travelling on a bus in Cockenzie, East Lothian on this date a group of men began singing 'The Sash', a song associated with the Orange movement. A Catholic by the name of Patrick Smith Connachan stood up and objected to the song, and was confronted by one of the group, a young naval rating named Walter Kerr. The two men departed the bus at the next stop, at the entrance to Whin Park, and began to fight. During the altercation Connachan was knocked to the ground, whereupon Kerr was said to have kicked him several times in the head and stamped his feet down on his face. Connachan died shortly afterwards from his injuries, while Kerr departed and boarded another bus. Arrested soon after, he was found guilty of culpable homicide and sentenced to two years' imprisonment.

24 AUGUST 1730

James Bradie, a bookbinder in the Luckenbooths, was murdered by a chimneysweep apparently hired by a group of young men to commit the deed.

25 AUGUST 1709

The trial of the Master of Burleigh for murder resulted in a sentence to be beheaded at the Mercat Cross in Edinburgh early the following year. The Master's crime shows the arrogance of the nobility of the time. He had fallen for a young peasant girl from his father's estates in Fife, and decided that he would marry. However, his friends decided instead to send him abroad to save him from making a marriage beneath himself. He declared before leaving that he would return and that if his love should marry in the meantime that he would take her husband's life. Returning some years later, he found the lady to be married to a schoolteacher from Inverkeithing by the name of Henry Stenhouse. Making good his promise he immediately challenged the man, and when he received a refusal, informed him that he would either fight or be shot down on the spot. When the man again refused, he carried out his threat. The young Master was not to meet his end on the appointed date, however. In the intervening period between sentence and execution, he escaped from the Tollbooth Gaol disguised in his sister's clothing. He lived until 1757, but, his property having been confiscated as a result of his flight, died a broken and destitute man.

26 AUGUST 1679

James Baillie, the 2nd Lord Forrester and Laird of Corstorphine, was known as a man who liked his drink, seldom paid his debts, and enjoyed the sins of the flesh a little too much. His philandering led him to take, as one of his many lovers, his own niece, a married woman by the name of Christian Nimmo. The pair met regularly in a dovecot by a sycamore tree in the grounds of Corstorphine Castle, but on this night when she came to the spot, not finding him present she had a servant fetch him from the Black Bull Inn. When he arrived he was considerably the worse for drink and a violent quarrel broke out, during which he called her a 'whoor'. Enraged by the insult, Nimmo grasped the sword from his side and ran him through with it. As he lay dying she ran and hid herself in the castle, but was soon found and taken to the Tollbooth to await trial. She twice attempted to avert her fate, first by feigning a pregnancy and later by escaping the prison dressed in men's clothing. But both were foiled and she was beheaded on 12 November. Since that time rumours have abounded that her spirit haunts the sycamore tree as a ghostly figure in white.

27 AUGUST 1819

Ralph Woodness was executed by hanging on this day for the crime of breaking into a haberdasher's shop and stealing stock worth between £350 and £400. The burglary had taken place on the night of 29 March in the company of a man named Richard Smith. The pair used a chisel to remove a shutter and a glass window from the front of the shop, and loaded all the goods onto a gig which they had hired for the purpose. Suspicion fell on them when they unloaded the goods in a public house in Glasgow and asked the publican to look after the stock until they returned. The publican's wife, being suspicious, called the police, who impounded the goods and arrested the pair. However, only Woodness was actually seen by witnesses handling the goods, and as such the case against Smith was found 'not proven'. The judge impressed upon him how lucky he had been to escape with his own life intact, and recommended he make an alteration in his ways if he wanted it to remain that way for very much longer.

28 AUGUST 1819

The *Scotsman* newspaper reported today that William Charlton, who had been found guilty of murder at Durham Assizes and sentenced to death, had, on arrival in Newcastle, been recognised by a woman working in that city as a prostitute, who had been present in 1812 when a spate of rioting had broken out in Edinburgh on Hogmanay. Three of the rioters had been executed for their part in these events, but during their trial had intimated that the whole had been organised and orchestrated by a man named Johnston, who had since fled to America. The police in Newcastle, it was said, sent to Edinburgh for a description of Johnston, and found that two distinguishing marks, a scar over the left eye and a peculiar mark on the leg, were present on their prisoner. Justice, it seems, had caught up with him at last.

29 AUGUST 1925

When 5-year-old John Mullen fell into 6ft of water in Leith Harbour while playing on Fish Quay, two men standing nearby rushed to the aid of the child. John Ormiston, a carter from Dublin Street, and John Poulson from East Cromwell Street both plunged into the water, mindless of their own safety. Poulson, who had previously lost one of his hands in an accident, was first to reach the boy and pulled him to the quayside steps and to safety. Ormiston, however, after entering the water, was seen to break the surface once in distress and then disappear back into its depths. It seems likely that he struck his head on something on diving into the harbour which knocked him insensible. The water causing him to drift, his body was finally discovered on the opposite side of the harbour early the following morning.

30 AUGUST 1929

Margaret Fraser, a married woman of Prestonpans, was not in the least suspicious when her lodger, Mary Holmes, returned home from meeting her mother-in-law together with her

3½-year-old son, but without her 2-month-old daughter. She had met Mrs Holmes' husband, a commercial traveller in Glasgow, and been told that the mother-in-law was concerned for the welfare of the children, and so when Mary told her that the baby had gone to Perth with the older woman, and that the boy was to go as well but would not travel without his mother, she was satisfied with this explanation. The evening was spent pleasantly with Mary playing dominoes with Mrs Fraser and her husband, and the following day Mrs Holmes and the boy departed and all seemed in order. However, a few weeks later, when reading in the newspaper of the body of a baby girl washed up on the beach, and recognising the description of the clothing, Mrs Fraser began to have suspicions, and on 21 September she was visited by the police and gave a statement. Two days later Mrs Holmes was arrested in Perthshire, where she had taken work as a housekeeper. In reply to the advertisement placed on 3 August, she had informed her employers about her son, but made no mention of a baby girl. The woman, it transpired, was unmarried and her real surname was Brackenridge. After her arrest she made a statement admitting that on the afternoon in question she had met with two women who wanted to adopt the infant, but feeling that they would not treat the child right, she had refused, and had then taken the girl to the shore and killed her. She was found guilty of culpable homicide, but a plea of insanity was accepted.

31 AUGUST 1888

Two accidental deaths in the Edinburgh region were reported in the newspapers on this date. In the first, a pit accident near Bathgate, a miner by the name of William Brown was severely injured when gunpowder exploded in his face. He sustained a fracture to the skull, severe burning and was blinded. He died in hospital the following day. Meanwhile, at the St Margaret's Works of the North British Railway Co., a joiner named Adam Cairns was crushed against a stone wall while fixing an iron hinge to the folding door of a wagon which, by some means, moved forward during the operation pinning him in place. The hinge he was fixing was pressed against his throat, and he died from asphyxiation before his fellow workmen were able to free him.

SEPTEMBER

❦✠❦

Baillie McMorran's house. (Author's Collection)

1 SEPTEMBER 1886

Three young boys were buried alive while playing in a sandpit at Beaver Bank. The bank had been undermined by workmen, and while the children played it gave way under them. One of the three, a boy named Wood, was pulled out unconscious but alive after ten minutes of digging, but the other two were not so lucky. Robby Morrison, aged 6, was dug out around twenty minutes later, but attempts to revive him were unsuccessful. The third child, 11-year-old Hugh Gordon, was not known to be involved until his mother noticed he was missing and Wood confirmed that he had also been present. His body was recovered half an hour later.

2 SEPTEMBER 1793

Shortly after midnight a gentleman returning to his home in St Andrew's Square saw, near his own home, a man severely beating a woman, and in chivalrous fashion swiftly went to her aid. As he did so another man appeared behind him, and then both men and the woman knocked him down and robbed him of all he had on him. The street squabble, it seemed, had been a ruse to ensnare any passing man with enough honour to rush to the defence of a stricken female.

3 SEPTEMBER 1791

Archibald Mathie and Robert Falconer, both carters, were tried in the High Court of Justiciary, accused of assault with intent to murder Roger Aytoun, a Writer to the Signet, and Lieutenant Alexander Home, an officer in the navy. The latter men had been travelling by coach from Peebles back to Edinburgh after a dinner when they found the road blocked by the unattended carts of the pair, laden with lead. Having to exit their coach in order to unblock the road, they decided as punishment to unload some of the lead from the carts onto the road. They then continued their journey, but when the two carters found what had been done, they took offence and chased after the men. Catching up with the coach they dragged the men out and began to beat and bludgeon them, to an extent that, according to the court, they would surely have killed them had it not been for the intervention of another man, John Martin, who arrived on the scene and prevented any further bloodshed. The men admitted the charge of assault but not the intent to murder, and so rather than plead guilty or not guilty they entered a plea to 'deny the libel as laid.' The jury, however, found them guilty on all charges and they were sentenced to be whipped through the streets of the city and banished from the kingdom for seven years.

4 SEPTEMBER 1937

A jury in Edinburgh this day returned a verdict of 'not proven' against Mark Hutchison, accused of culpable homicide after a fight the previous April. The incident appears to have begun in a restaurant when Ronald Crawford jostled Peter Hutchison, the brother of the accused man. Hutchison attempted to leave the scene, but Crawford followed him to his home, continuing to punch and kick out at him. On arrival at his house, his brother came out to see what was the matter, and joined in the fight. During the altercation it was said that Crawford received a knee to the abdomen, which was the cause of his death some eleven days later. However, Peter Hutchison testified in court that he might have caused the death rather than his brother, but that he did not know. The jury seemed to have been swayed by this, and the fact that the deceased man appeared to be the cause of the fight in the first place.

The scene of the Mauricewood pit disaster. (Author's Collection)

5 SEPTEMBER 1889

The Mauricewood Pit Disaster remains one of the worst accidental tragedies in Scottish history. The pit, near Peniciuk to the south of Edinburgh, operated on two levels, an iron seam at eighty fathoms and a coal seam at 160 fathoms. On the day of the disaster there were seventy men working underground, sixty-three of whom lost their lives. The mine was operated by the Shotts Iron Co., who were afterwards heavily criticised for their safety procedures. According to law every colliery pit had to have at least two shafts for exit, however in the case of Mauricewood the second exit, nearby Greenlaw Pit, was in the opposite direction of the main shaft from the work face, making it next to useless to the men trapped underground when fire broke out in the engine house of the shaft at around 12.30 p.m. A few men escaped during the early part of the fire, and with water being sent down to flood the pit there was hope that others could be rescued. But that hope began to fade when a lift carriage was sent down and brought up four men, three of whom died from smoke inhalation on the journey while the fourth expired shortly afterwards. The following day rescue workers began to penetrate the shafts but found only dead bodies, and the decision was taken shortly afterwards to seal up the pit and allow the fire to burn itself out.

6 SEPTEMBER 1730

The dead body of an infant was found on this day in the Canongate Churchyard, placed inside a wigmaker's box. The evidence of the body suggested that the child had been murdered, rather than stillborn or having died from natural causes.

7 SEPTEMBER 1763

Captain Porteous, of the City Guard, having been found guilty of murder for firing into an unruly crowd at the hanging of Andrew Wilson on 14 April, was condemned to be hanged on 8 September. Porteous had powerful friends, and many in authority were made nervous by the sentence, fearing it set a precedent and that their own decisions might result in prosecution. Consequently a petition for clemency was quickly drawn up to be presented to the monarch, and in the meantime, on 28 August, Parliament granted a stay of six weeks' duration on the execution. Indignation within the city at this move was intense. Porteous had been a hated figure even before the events with which he was charged, and it was felt by the general population that the punishment was thoroughly deserved. Now they feared

Captain Porteous is strung up by rioters. (Mary Evans Picture Library)

that the man would eventually escape justice altogether, and a plan was drawn up to ensure that this would not be the case. On the evening of the 7th they rose up in a mob, quickly seizing the city gates and securing them against all comers. Marching on the Tollbooth Gaol, they were initially opposed by the magistrates and others in authority, but refused to submit. Finding the gaol doors barred against them, they burned them down and entered, heading straight for Porteous's cell, where they found the man hiding in the chimney and pleading for his life. Ignoring his cries, he was seized and marched straight to the Grassmarket. Along the way a shop was broken into and a length of rope obtained, the rioters leaving a guinea on the shop counter as proper payment for the goods. Arriving at the execution place, the rope was quickly attached to a dyer's pole and Porteous was strung up while the crowd cheered his fate. Then, having first checked to ensure that he was indeed dead, the whole assembly dispersed and went peaceably back to their homes. Although strenuous efforts were made to find out the ringleaders of the plot, in the end no action was taken and no punishment ever meted out.

8 SEPTEMBER 1568

A pestilence broke out in Edinburgh, said to have been brought in by a merchant named James Dalgliesh. Families infected were made to move out of their homes into hastily erected shacks on the Burgh Muir. Failure to do so was punishable by death. In the meanwhile their clothes were purified by boiling and their houses disinfected by officers of the city, who were appointed at a salary of £8 monthly, while special buriers of the dead were also employed at £5 monthly. These people were all given a grey cloth uniform featuring the cross of St Andrew to wear to distinguish them from the general population. The sickness lasted until the following February and was said to have taken the lives of around 2,500 inhabitants, nearly one tenth of the population at that time.

9 SEPTEMBER 1630

The basis for laws regarding incest in most European nations are centred around the biblical passage *Leviticus 18: 6–18*, in which God passes down instruction to Moses regarding with whom it is forbidden to have sexual relations. This passage is not entirely clear and the rules are often confused. It was through such a confused reading that Alexander Blair, a tailor from Currie, a small village now swallowed up by the outskirts of Edinburgh, was on this day beheaded for the crime of incest for marrying his first wife's half-brother's daughter who, clearly, was no actual blood relation of his whatsoever.

10 SEPTEMBER: Medieval Edinburgh

Entertainment was a rare commodity in the old town. Unlike in London, theatre in Edinburgh was generally a treat for the educated classes, when it was allowed at all. For the common worker, a public torture or execution was always a big draw, and the Robin Hood Festivals were a treat until they were forbidden. One entertainment that always attracted a large crowd was the Italian Flyer. Not necessarily always the same person, the Italian Flyer was a tightrope walker who would string his rope between the steeples of churches and cross unharnassed and with no safety net. Unfortunately, the trick tended to lead to many imitations, and stories of men and boys plunging to untimely deaths while trying to emulate the act are numerous.

11 SEPTEMBER 1826

While walking down the West Port, a young man named Bain, a hatter, accidentally knocked into an elderly lady, causing her to fall. Her son, walking with her, was about to take action at this perceived affront to his mother, when another man by the name of Scoullar came rushing from a nearby inn shouting 'Let me to him, I'll do his business,' and struck Bain a blow that killed him on the spot.

12 SEPTEMBER 1678

For most women up until this period, a charge of witchcraft had essentially been a death sentence. The accusers would torture the poor unfortunate until a confession had been extracted. The case of Katherine Liddell of Prestonpans in East Lothian is an interesting alternative. Liddell had been taken by John Rutherford, the Baillie of that town, on suspicion of witchcraft and had, over a period of six weeks, been subjected to a veritable barrage of ill treatment by that man and other associates. Among other abuses she was subjected to were many nights of sleep deprivation, and the pricking of pins into various parts of her body with the loss of a great quantity of blood until it was said that there was little of her skin that was not raised, and the flesh swelled, and that she was close to death. However, the woman must have been made of stern stuff, for not only did she withstand all tortures without making any false self-accusations, but she managed to have a petition presented before the Privy Council, charging her captors with defamation, false imprisonment and open and manifest oppression. On hearing the evidence, the council pronounced Liddell entirely innocent of the charges she had been accused of, and condemned Rutherford and his associates, although letting off all but one, David Cowan 'the pricker', without punishment.

13 SEPTEMBER 1831

When Alexander Dalziel, a farmer from Drylaw, met a man standing in the road in Inverleith, he realised there was something not right about him. The man stood stock still with his arm outstretched holding a small table fork, and remained in that position for some time before going into a nearby field, kneeling down and proclaiming himself to be William Wallace. Dalziel was correct in his assumption that the man was insane, but what he was unaware of was that he had recently used the fork to murder his own 8-year-old son. George Waters, a ship's carpenter, had returned home that afternoon and, finding his wife and child absent, had gone out and found the boy playing with the fork with some friends. Telling his son that they were going to visit an aunt in Northumberland Street, they had set off towards Stockbridge, but, on passing the field, Waters had struck the child on the head with the butt end of the fork and then begun repeatedly stabbing him in the chest with it until he was dead. No explanation for this action was forthcoming and, found to be outside his senses, he was ordered to be detained in an asylum for the remainder of his life.

14 SEPTEMBER 1938

While under the influence of excessive drink, Samuel McDougall, working on a gantry erected near Meadow Bridge in Seafield, drove his travelling crane over the edge of the gantry and into the sea. He was described as driving recklessly and at excessive speed, and cost the life of William McAndrew who was sat on the crane at the time. Steel plates had been attached to the end of the gantry to prevent such an accident, but they were only capable of stopping the crane if it had been moving at its usual speed of 3mph or 4mph, and not one travelling at the speed at which McDougall was driving it. He was sentenced to six months in prison, the judge stating that the larger part of his punishment was that he would never be trusted to work in his chosen profession again.

15 SEPTEMBER 1595

Rebellious teenagers are, it seems, an age-old problem. Having had part of their annual holiday curtailed, on the evening of 13 September 1595 the students of Edinburgh High School broke into their schoolhouse with guns and other weapons and barricaded themselves in, in protest at their treatment. They remained there, holed up, for the whole of the following day, and on the 15th the council sent Baillie John McMorran, who sometimes taught at the school, together with a posse of officers to end the dispute. When the students refused all entreaties to open the doors of the school, McMorran and the other officers attempted to prise open the back door. On this occurring, one of the students by the name of Sinclair thrust a gun through the window and ordered them to leave or, by God, he would put a bullet through somebody's head. The men, believing that the youngsters would not dare shoot,

Edinburgh High School. (Author's Collection)

continued with their work, whereupon Sinclair fired. The bullet striking McMorran clean in the forehead, he fell to the ground dead on the instant.

16 SEPTEMBER 1843

Under the heading 'Sudden Death in the police office', the *Scotsman* reported that a man named Alexander Henderson, a porter from Leith Walk, 'was discovered by a policeman lying drunk in a stair in Blair Street, and carried to the police office, where he was put into a cell. He was then able to speak, but was considerably the worse of drink. In about two hours he was found dead, it is supposed from apoplexy.'

17 SEPTEMBER 1876

Alexander Murray was a man with a troubled mind. His marble and slate business, into which he had ploughed all his savings, was failing, and his baby daughter had been born with an eye defect which meant she needed constant attention day and night, so that for several weeks he had had little more than an hour or two sleep each night. It was in this state of mind that Murray, said by friends and family to have been formerly the most pleasant natured of people, took an axe and split open the heads of both of his children, a boy aged 5 and his 14-month-old daughter, in their home in Rosslyn Street. Having completed the deed, Murray carefully washed the axe, and, walking quite calmly to the nearby Leith branch line, placed his head on the railway track in front of an oncoming train and allowed it to decapitate him.

18 SEPTEMBER 1915

William Juta, a 25-year-old South African medical student at Edinburgh University, was well known in the South African Union in Buccleuch Place, and so it was no surprise when he arrived there at 10 p.m. on the night of 17 September. He stayed for a while in the library of the club, and then went to one of the upstairs rooms in the building. Moments later the sound of a shot being fired was heard, and the caretaker of the club hurried to the room where he found Juta lying on the floor with a bullet hole above his right ear and a revolver still clutched in his right hand. A doctor was summoned, but the man was already dead. Inspection of the room turned up a set of keys and a letter placed on the table. In the letter Juta stated that he had shot his wife, child and mother-in-law and had come to the Union to take his own life, wishing to die among friends. He also gave instructions for his and his family's burial. Police were called and arrived at the address given in Falcon Avenue, Morningside, in the early hours of the 18th, where they found the scene as described. The man's wife and 4-year-old child were found shot in their bed, while the mother-in-law was found to have been up and about but was evidently taken by surprise as no signs of a struggle were present.

19 SEPTEMBER 1929

When Richard Antonius Steen, a retired marine engineer, decided to take his own life, he clearly decided that the event should be highly organised. Consequently he hailed a horse-drawn cab on Princes' Street and asked the driver what the fare would be to the Royal Infirmary. On being informed of the price, he paid the man in advance, and asked him to wait while he posted a letter. On his return, the man took his seat inside the cab, and they set off up the mound where, just as they were passing the Bank of Scotland building, the driver heard a muffled explosion. However, he thought nothing of this, assuming that the sound came from a nearby motorcar. On arrival at the infirmary he found that Mr Steen had departed this life with the aid of a six-chambered revolver. Steen had ensured that his driver should encounter the minimum inconvenience, having been paid the correct amount for the journey, and the location to which he had been driven meaning that his remains could be quickly removed and taken to the mortuary inside. The letter he had posted had contained instructions to settle his final affairs.

20 SEPTEMBER 1580

Returning from Danzig with a large cargo and seven prominent local businessmen on board, plague broke out on board the *William*, a ship belonging to Captain John Downie, while in the Firth of Forth. By order of the Privy Council, the ship was forced to land at St Colm's Inch, an island in the Firth, where the crew and passengers had to remain on pain of death until the plague had run its course. They remained until 27 November, during which the captain, several seamen and a number of the passengers died, and much of the cargo was spoiled.

21 SEPTEMBER 1745

Prestonpans, a small coastal town to the east of Edinburgh was, on this day, the scene of the first significant battle of the Jacobite uprising. Five days earlier, Bonnie Prince Charlie had marched into the city at the head of his army and taken control of the area. The government response was to raise a force against him, under Sir John Cope. The battle lasted barely fifteen minutes, Cope's inexperienced troops panicking under a frontal assault by the fierce highlanders, and around 400 government troops were killed and another 1,500 wounded or taken prisoner, while Jacobite losses were said to be less than 100.

*Charles Edward Stuart, Bonnie
Prince Charlie. (Author's Collection)*

22 SEPTEMBER 1791

In a sequel to the sentence passed on Archibald Mathie and Robert Falconer on the 3rd of this month, the public executioner, John High, was placed in the Black Hole, a windowless cell in the Tollbooth Gaol, and spent 24-hours there as punishment for not performing his duty adequately while whipping the two men through the streets. On being set at liberty again on this date he was warned by the magistrate that should he be found guilty of similar neglect in the future he would be shown how the job should be done by being whipped through the streets himself.

23 SEPTEMBER 1865

When ship's engineer Isaac Beamish was paid off by Luke Scott, captain of the steamer *Xantha* on which he had been working, he refused to accept that the misconduct of which he had been accused was as serious an offence as had been implied. He therefore took the matter to solicitors, who obtained a better deal for him. However, he still seems to have felt that he deserved more, and on this night took a cab to Leith docks where he threatened Scott with a gun if he would not come with him to his solicitor's office for further negotiation. When Scott refused, Beamish fired the pistol at him, but the first two shots misfired and Scott took to his heels, pursued by Beamish whose third shot fired but missed. The man then returned to the cab and attempted thereby to make his escape, but was followed by a policeman and another sailor, who, between them, disarmed him and took him into custody.

24 SEPTEMBER 1570

John Kello was a young man of humble origins but ambitious for the best position he could attain in life. Taking a post in the Presbyterian ministry, he was appointed parson of the small parish of Spott in East Lothian in 1560. Having taken a wife, Margaret Thomson, from his own lowly class, to all intents and purposes they settled down as a happy couple in their new life. He fathered three children by his wife, and she seemed always content and loving in his company. But Kello was still ambitious for more and, after speculating on an investment which returned a healthy profit, he began to plan for a brighter future. Unfortunately, further investments did not prove so successful, and he began to accumulate debt, and at this time he got it into his mind that if he were not married then he might pursue a more advantageous union with the daughter of the local laird. Waiting his opportunity, he found it one Sunday morning while his wife knelt in her devotions. Having first carefully spread rumours that she suffered terribly from night terrors, he strangled her with a towel, and then hung the body from a hook in the ceiling of her own room to make her death appear to be a suicide. Then he exited the house, using the back entrance and leaving the front door locked and the keys inside, and went immediately to the kirk to conduct the morning service. After service he arranged for others to accompany him home to visit his wife, in order to have witnesses to his 'discovery' of the body. His act of grief appears to have convinced the local community, and he might have escaped justice, but when he decided to visit a fellow minister in Dunbar to receive counselling on his misfortune, Andrew Simpson, the minister in question seems to have become suspicious of his manner. Recounting a dream Kello had once described to him, he attributed it to a guilty mind and him of being the author of his wife's death. After wrestling with his own conscience, Kello eventually travelled to Edinburgh where he made a full confession of his crime before a judge.

25 SEPTEMBER 1835

They say you can choose your friends but you can't choose your family. A young servant working in the New Town probably wished on this date that you could. Having left her position earlier in the week, her mother had become alarmed that she did not come to her home, and feared that she had been seduced and led astray. She therefore went to the former employer asking for his assistance in locating the girl, and the police were called. An officer went in search of the girl and succeeded in locating her in a lodging house. However, the cagey manner in which she submitted to his questions roused suspicions, and he decided to search her room whereupon he found numerous items of value belonging to her former mistress, which the family, up until that point, had failed to notice were missing.

26 SEPTEMBER 1728

A salutary tale appeared in the *Edinburgh Evening Courant* on this date: 'A man coming from Leith some nights ago pretty late was attacked by some rogues and robbed, but finding nothing about him but sixpence they beat him most severely. A warning for people to come home more timeously, or to keep more money in their pockets!'

27 SEPTEMBER 1837

The *Scotsman* newspaper reported that on this date 'the mutilated body of a male child, about nine months old, in a state of decomposition, was discovered in a plantation belonging to Dr Monro, in the parish of Colinton. From appearances it had lain there for about a month, and it is thought foul play had been used by some unnatural wretch. The head was severed from the body, as was also the left arm. It was removed to Colinton session-house, where it now lies, and exertions are making to discover to whom it belonged.' Dr Monro was the anatomy professor at Edinburgh University to whom Burke and Hare had originally intended to sell their first body.

Colinton. (Author's Collection)

28 SEPTEMBER: Medieval Edinburgh

In medieval Edinburgh the burden of bankruptcy was made visible for all to see. In order to be released from the debtor's prison, the bankrupt had to agree to abide by certain rules. Firstly he had to provide, at his own expense, a flat yellow cap. Then, during the time he was working to pay off his debts, he was required to spend each day from ten in the morning until one in the afternoon, sitting on a pillory rock of hewn stone at the Mercat Cross wearing the cap so that all would see his shame. Punishment for failure to attend was immediate arrest and return to prison.

29 SEPTEMBER 1827

The *Scotsman* reported on a serious accident that had occurred near Libberton Dams. A Dr Barker of York Place had been returning to Edinburgh in a double-seated gig together with three companions when a woman, on hearing the sound of the horses and attempting to clear the road, ran in front and was knocked down by the lead horse. Frightened by the incident, the horse bolted, causing the gig to overturn and the passengers to be thrown out onto the road, injuring Dr Barker so badly that his leg was amputated the following morning.

30 SEPTEMBER 1652

A description of the kind of inhuman treatment of criminals carried out for the least of crimes can be found in this quote from the diary of John Nicoll during the time of Cromwell's rule: 'Last of September – Two Englishmen, for drinking the King's health, were taken and bound at Edinburgh Cross, where either of them received thirty-nine whips on their naked backs and shoulders, thereafter their lugs [ears] were nailed to the gallows. One had his lug cut from the right with a razor, the other also being nailed to the gibbet had his mouth skobit [pierced with an adze] and his tongue being drawn out the full length was bound together betwixt two sticks, hard together, with a skanzie-thread for the space of half one hour thereby.'

OCTOBER

✠

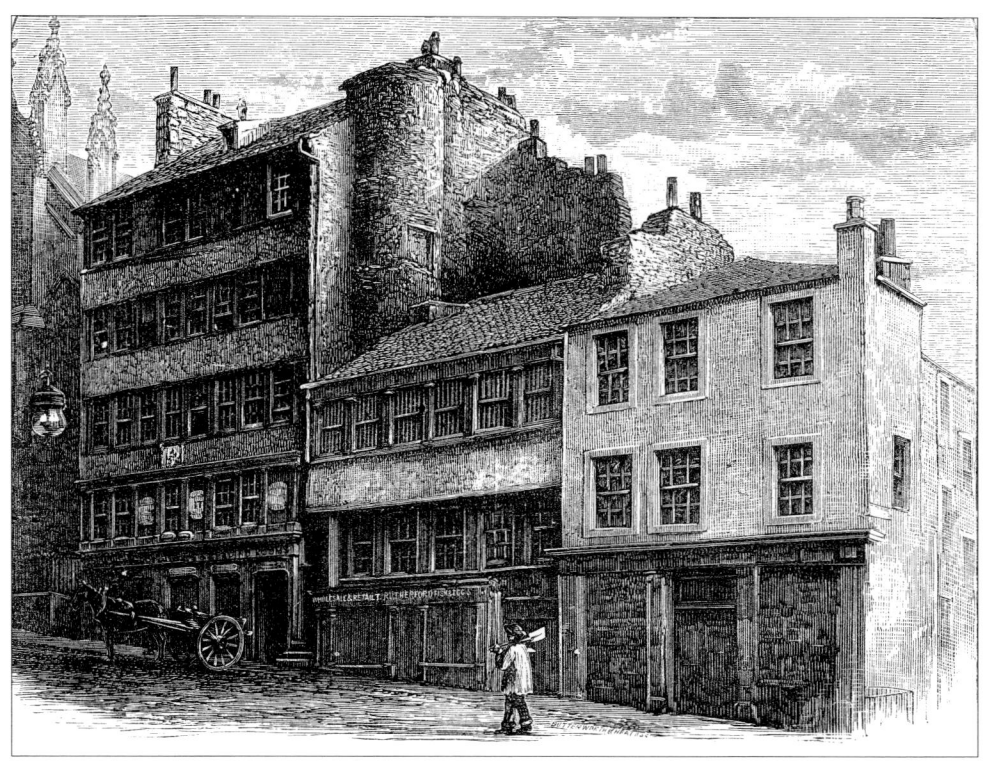

Canongate Excise Office, scene of Deacon William Brodie's final burglary. (Author's Collection)

1 OCTOBER 1788

This day saw the end of the career of one of the most notorious villains in Edinburgh's history. Deacon William Brodie has gone down in history not merely for his crimes, but also as the inspiration behind Robert Louis Stevenson's novel *Dr Jekyll and Mr Hyde*, for he was one of the city's most respected citizens during the day, but at night he consorted with the lowest of its inhabitants in an orgy of drinking, gambling and fornication. To fund this lifestyle he took to burglary. As a skilled wood-worker and a pillar of the community, and as Deacon of

the Guild of Wrights and Masons, Brodie was frequently entrusted with the keys to the great houses in which he worked. He would make wax impressions of these, and then return at a later date to let himself and his accomplices inside to relieve his patrons of their riches. Brodie enjoyed a long and successful career in crime, and is said to have stolen the silver mace of Edinburgh University, which went missing around this time, for no reason other than to prove that he could. But eventually fate caught up with him in the shape of a botched raid on the Excise Office. Although escaping himself, one of his cohorts, Andrew Ainslie, was captured and turned Kings Evidence. Brodie fled the city to Amsterdam, but was apprehended there and extradited back to face trial. He was executed on this date alongside another member of the gang, George Smith, supposedly on a gallows built by his own hands. The fourth member, John Brown, who already had a death sentence hanging over his head in England, had made an agreement with the Crown to give evidence in return for a free pardon.

Deacon William Brodie and George Smith. (Author's Collection)

2 OCTOBER 1716

It is wise for gentlemen to be discrete about their extra-marital affairs. Captain John Cayley, an Englishman who had arrived in Edinburgh as a commissioner of his majesty's customs, embarked on a dalliance with Mrs McFarlane, wife of one of Edinburgh's more prominent public officials. However, the young man was unable to keep matters to himself and, while in drink, let slip the information which quickly became a scandal within the local society. On the date in question, his injudiciousness having come to her attention, when he came to visit the lady in her chambers, she led him to the bedroom where he presumably expected to enjoy an afternoon in her bounteous embrace. Instead he found himself facing a pair of loaded pistols that he himself had loaned to her husband a few days earlier. A moment later he was dead, the shot from the first pistol having merely gone through his hand, but the second having penetrated his heart. Following her action she calmly locked the bedroom door and sent a servant to fetch her husband, who was away at his business. He, equally calmly, gathered together what money he could muster and conveyed her out of the city to safety, returning himself a day or so later to declare at court that he had had no foreknowledge of her plans.

3 OCTOBER 1728

A group of lads were drinking and carousing in an alehouse in the Canongate on this evening. As the hour grew later so the group grew to be more intoxicated and much louder and more raucous in their behaviour. Eventually, one of the other customers grew tired of their display, and instructed them that it was time that they left for home or else he would call the guard. The group, being in no mind to take orders, set on the man and beat him severely, dragging him into the cellar and continuing the beating until they believed him dead. The man, sensible of the danger he was in, chose not to disavow them of this belief, but lay as still as possible, and during the next few moments heard one of the group suggest that they kill the landlord also for allowing the man to speak to them in such a way, but another argued that one murder was enough for one night, and the group departed.

4 OCTOBER 1793

A group of Army deserters lodged in the Tollbooth Gaol were to be treated on this night to a meal of broth carried up to them by a woman and said to come from a nearby inn. The flagon, it transpired, contained strong spirits and not broth, and before long the men were extremely intoxicated and making a great deal of noise. The keeper, investigating the din, entered the room and was immediately knocked down and nearly killed by the men who saw this as their opportunity to escape. Fortunately for the keeper two other men had gone with him, and they managed to enlist the aid of some other prisoners who had been confined for debt, and between them they were able to bring the situation back under control.

5 OCTOBER 1874

A seaman named Edward Broadley pleaded guilty in the Sheriff's Court on this day to having beaten his wife with a cane on the upper part of her body, in their house in Kirkgate, Leith. The man was found to have no fewer than nine previous convictions for assaulting his wife recorded against him. The Sheriff, remarking on the cowardly nature of the act, sentenced the prisoner to nine months' hard labour.

6 OCTOBER 1886

The *Scotsman* reported on a speech given by the Revd Richard Baxter, editor of the *Christian Herald*, at the Freemason's Hall in George Street. During the speech, Baxter prophesied the destruction of Edinburgh in a series of three earthquakes, to take place in 1896, 1900 and 1901, during which every wall of the city would fall to the ground. He also prophesied that Christ's second coming would occur in 1896, and that what would follow would be 'dreadful wars, revolutions, famines, pestilences, and the rise of Napoleon as the great military, democratic, despotic, red-Republican, socialist anti-Christ, to world-wide dominion for three-and-a-half years ... with the massacre of millions of Christians for refusing to receive his mark.'

7 OCTOBER 1828: The West Port Murders

Some time at the beginning of October things began to unravel for Burke and Hare. They had committed one more murder since the summer; that of a charwoman named Mrs Hostler. But now, like they had with Mary Paterson, they chose another unwise victim. James Wilson was a mentally deficient teenager who lived and begged on the streets

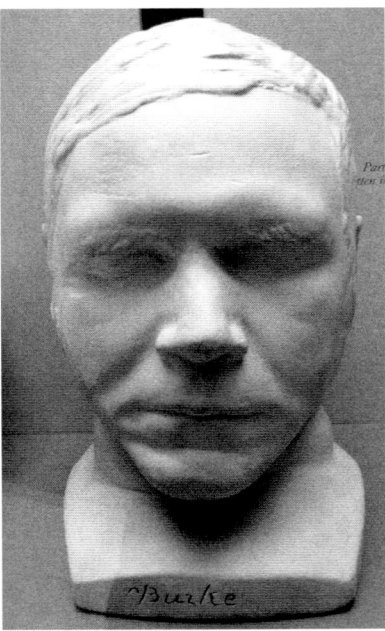

The death mask of William Burke in the Royal College of Surgeons Museum. (Author's Collection)

of the city and had become a well-loved local figure, referred to by all who knew him as 'Daft Jamie'. It was Maggie Hare on this occasion who did the enticing, and, after bringing him back to the house, she went and fetched Burke from Rymer's grog shop. The two men then led him into the back room where Burke and his wife had formerly slept, and tried to entice him with whisky in the usual way, but Jamie was reluctant to drink too much. Finally growing impatient, Hare jumped on him and began to suffocate him, and Burke had no choice but to join in. Jamie was big and powerful and put up a tremendous struggle, but eventually the force of the two men overcame him. The problem, of course, was that as soon as the body was delivered to Surgeon's Square, Dr Knox's assistants recognised the corpse, as he was such a familiar figure about town. When he saw the body, Dr Knox denied that it was that of Jamie, but quickly decided to sever the head and the feet (which were highly distinctive as the boy had a deformity).

8 OCTOBER 1828

The Police Court listings of the *Scotsman* for this date included the story of a 'stout young man' convicted of aggravated assault against a number of individuals. The incident began when a woman was seen running down the High Street screaming murder and imploring people to protect her. Finally exhausted, she tried to take refuge in a doorway, but her pursuer caught her and began to rain blows down on her. One man who tried to intervene was immediately knocked unconscious, and another who attempted to remonstrate with him was punched so hard in the mouth that one of his teeth was knocked out. On sentencing the man to sixty days' imprisonment, the magistrate expressed regret that he was not permitted to be more severe.

9 OCTOBER 1730

At John McPharline's lodging house in the Timber Bush in Leith, a woman arrived from York and took a room. Seeming in good health, she ate her evening meal and then retired for the night. The following morning, when she did not arise, her chamber was entered and she was found to be dead. It was later discovered that she was seven months pregnant, and that the father of the child was not her husband, under which circumstances it was presumed that she had poisoned herself rather than bear the shame.

10 OCTOBER 1681

A common method of disposing of unwanted prisoners was to take them into the armed forces. When it was proposed that six Covenanters, one of whom, Robert Garnock, had been in prison for at least three years at this point, should be pressed into service in Spain, the men were taken before the council, but there refused all authority of the King and were sent instead to trial for treason. Five of the men, Garnock among them, were found guilty and sentenced to be hanged. Another of the five, Patrick Forman, was also to have his hand struck off prior to execution for possessing a knife engraved with the words 'This is to cut the throat of tyrants.' Together with the remaining three, David Ferrie, James Stuart and Alexander Russell, the execution was carried out as planned on this date, and then their heads were removed and displayed on pikes at the Pleasance Port, while their bodies were buried at the foot of the gallows. However, a zealous young Covenanter named James Renwick decided to gather together a group of like-minded friends, and by night they exhumed the bodies and removed them to the West Kirkyard where they carried out a proper Christian burial. The heads and Forman's hand were also removed, but being scared to cross the city with these items they were hidden separately, with the intent to eventually reunite them with their rightful owners.

11 OCTOBER 1830

Children playing in Baxter's Close off the Lawnmarket on this day noticed something unusual about the property belonging to a well-known local character who went commonly by the name of 'Pig Willie'. The man, whose real name was Alexander Mackay, was a wandering seller of crockery and as such was often away from his home. For this reason, his neighbours had paid no attention to the fact that he had not been seen for about three months. When the police forced the door and went inside they found the bodies of Willie and his faithful dog, both of whom had clearly been laying there for some considerable time and had been partially consumed by rats.

12 OCTOBER 1790

David Currie, the publican of an alehouse at Bridge End in Dalkieth, and his wife were overcome by the smoke of sulphurous coal during the night as the result of a blocked flue. By the time they were found Currie was close to death, and he expired shortly thereafter. His wife lingered for a day before joining him in his fate. The couple had been married for nearly fifty years and between them had produced twenty-two children.

13 OCTOBER 1972

In the early afternoon of this day, 18-year-old Helga Konrad, a shy farmer's daughter from Schwerbach, Germany, married her Dutch sweetheart, Ernst Dumoulin, in a registry-office wedding in Edinburgh. By nine o'clock that evening her dead body lay at the foot of Salisbury Crags, apparently slain by his hand in order to obtain insurance money on her life.

Salisbury Crags. (Author's Collection)

The pair had arrived in Edinburgh on 19 September after absconding from her father's farm. They stayed at a lodging house at 8 Torpichan Street where the landlord, Mr Herbert Wood, gave evidence that they had resided in the country for the required fifteen days to obtain a marriage license. It later transpired that Dumoulin had several scams on the go, including two insurance policies on his wife, both of which turned out to be invalid, and an attempt to defraud the Bank of Nova Scotia out of £10,000. He had also stolen a car, which he sold to fund their journey to Scotland. He evidently planned the murder well in advance, but failed to properly read the insurance policy from which he hoped to claim £200,000, as he was told by their agent that it was invalidated because the accident occurred on a mountain and thus constituted a dangerous activity. After originally claiming that his wife merely slipped and fell, he later stated that Helga had been trying to push him from the cliff at the time of the accident. Either way, doctors challenged his claim that she slipped on the grounds that the cliff face was sloped and that had she fallen she would have grazed the face of the crags and sustained a great deal more skin damage, and therefore she must have gone over the edge with some force. Found guilty of murder, Dumoulin was sentenced to life imprisonment.

14 OCTOBER 1485

Although there is some dispute around the date, and many books list the event as occurring in 1479, this is the most probable date of the daring escape of Alexander, Duke of Albany, from Edinburgh Castle. Albany, the brother of King James III, had been arrested and imprisoned for a campaign of insurrection in the border areas, the aim of which was ultimately to unthrone his elder sibling and take the crown for himself. On the day in question he received two jugs of malvoisie wine from a ship berthed off Leith, which were passed into his cell unexamined. In the bottom of one flagon was a strong rope, and in the other a waxen roll containing a letter urging his escape and informing him that the King had resolved to execute him on the following morning. Inviting the captain of the guard and his three men to drink the wine with him, he contrived to intoxicate them while himself remaining quite sober. Having brought about this insensible state in them, without warning he seized the captain's dagger and dispatched the four men, throwing their bodies into the fire that blazed in the fireplace. Together with his own servant, they found a suitable spot and affixed the rope. The servant descended first, but the rope proved too short and he fell the last part of the way, knocking himself insensible and breaking his thigh. Rushing back to his bedchamber,

Albany brought the sheets from the bed and added them to the rope before lowering himself down to the foot of the rock and, lifting his stricken attendant onto his shoulders, he proceeded to walk the two miles to Leith where they boarded the waiting ship to safety.

15 OCTOBER 1938

Police were called after a street brawl between James McDermott and his brother Hendry, which left the latter beat to such an extent that he later died from his injuries. McDermott was taken into custody and charged with murder by the Sheriff's Court, but the charges were eventually dropped on the grounds that it was impossible to assign blame for the fight to either party.

16 OCTOBER 1856

The death of Margaret Darling after a long illness on this date sparked what was to become a highly celebrated court case. Dionysius Wielobycki was born in Poland and came to Edinburgh to study medicine. Obtaining his doctorate, he became a private practitioner and began ministering to the Darling family. Finding the family weak-willed and easily led, he convinced them to allow him also to attend to their business affairs, and to lodge all of their money in his hands as he would get them a better return on investments than previously. The money at that time was in the hands of the eldest brother, Thomas, but when he died it passed to his two living sisters, Margaret and Isabella, with none being set aside for his nieces and nephews, the children of two deceased sisters. With Margaret being seriously ill, Wielobycki enquired as to whether she would need to make a will in order for her money to pass into Isabella's hands, and thus remain under his control, and was told that Thomas' instructions should be sufficient. However, on her death it transpired that the nieces and nephews had a valid case to inherit. The day after this was established, it further transpired that Margaret had made a will after all, lodging all of her estate with her sister and under the doctor's control. The will was, of course, a hasty and ill-executed forgery and was quickly exposed. Until a few years earlier, forging a will had been a capital offence, and although this had been rescinded it was still considered one of the most heinous of crimes, and the trial was a sensation of its day. Wielobycki was found guilty on all charges and sentenced to be transported for fourteen years.

17 OCTOBER 1720

The murder of his wife by Nichol Muschat gained notoriety after Sir Walter Scott made reference to the case in his novel *The Heart of Midlothian*. However, while that book was fictional, the story itself was real. Muschat, a surgeon by training, having been married by arrangement and feeling no affection towards his wife, became enamoured of another and wanted to be rid of what he saw as an encumbrance on his happy life. Together with a man named Campbell, they planned to implicate Muschat's wife in adultery so that he could obtain a divorce, but this scheme came to nothing. They then attempted poison her, but either used an insufficient quantity or an inappropriate substance because it seemed to have little effect on the woman. Another scheme involved hiring a man to bludgeon her to death in Dickson's Close, but this scheme also fizzled out after they paid the man only a small portion of the money he had asked. Then, one night, while walking together to Duddingston and crossing the Royal Park, Muschat realised that he had the perfect opportunity to perform the deed himself out of sight of all witnesses. So, drawing a knife, he slit her throat and left her dead on the spot, running to his brother's house to confess what he had done. The next morning

The title of Sir Walter Scott's novel The Heart of Midlothian *refers to the old nickname for the Tollbooth Gaol. The spot where the door once stood is now marked by an actual heart picked into the paving stones and referred to by the same name. Visitors are encouraged to spit on the heart in the same way that the city folk used to spit on the door of the gaol. (Author's Collection)*

the body was found, the neck cut right down to the bone and other wounds about the body showing that a struggle had occurred. Muschat was seized and, his conscience weighing heavily on him, immediately confessed his crime and the whole scheme. He was sentenced to be hanged, and Campbell was declared infamous and banished. A cairn, known as Muschat's Cairn, was built on the spot where the murder occurred and provides the location for a fateful meeting in Scott's novel.

18 OCTOBER 1715

A letter of this date, written by the Revd J. Williamson of Musselburgh, tells the tale of 'the lamentable murder of Dr Rule last week by Craigmilar's second son, and the melancholy providence of a jeweller's servant, who was under some dejection for some time, and did, on Monday last, immediately after sermon, at Leith, run into the sea deliberately, and drown himself.'

19 OCTOBER 1726

On 7 October of this year, while digging in his garden in Lauriston, a man named Shaw discovered a wooden box buried in the soil, inside were the skulls of five men together with the bones of a hand. These were the heads of the Covenanters: Garnock, Forman, Ferrie, Stuart and Russell, executed forty-five years earlier on 10 October 1861. Laying the relics out in his summerhouse, Shaw gathered supporters of the old cause and it was determined to reunite the skulls with their other remains. A burial party was gathered, and on this date the graves in the West Kirkyard were opened and the skulls fitted to the bodies according to size. The bodies were then taken through the streets to the Greyfriars Kirkyard, where they were re-interred whole in the Martyr's Tomb in front of a large crowd.

The Martyr's Monument in Greyfriars Kirkyard. (Author's Collection)

20 OCTOBER 1827

Reported in the *Scotsman*: 'Susan Hutchison, a poor woman, residing in Bull's Close, Canongate, was delivered of a child about a week ago, which is since dead. None of her neighbours having seen her on Sunday, her house was entered, when she was found dead on the floor in the most wretched state of poverty. This poor creature had not even a blanket to cover her; and the cause of her death is believed to have arisen entirely from starvation.'

21 OCTOBER 1927

Ms Flora Kerr, a 23-year-old laundry worker, was charged on this day with the murder of her mother on 21 July by stabbing or cutting her in the neck with a knife. Evidence presented showed that Ms Kerr had a bad home life with her mother, who was constantly drunk and regularly abused her daughter with obscene language. During an argument which ensued after Ms Kerr returned home from a dance at around 10.30 p.m. on the night in question, the young girl had, on an impulse, picked up a kitchen knife and thrown it. Evidence being accepted that the woman's mother had been about to attack her with a metal bowl at the time, and previous convictions for drunk and disorderly behaviour and cruelty to children being taken into account, a plea of self-defence was accepted and Ms Kerr was found not guilty.

22 OCTOBER 1853

When William Cumming returned from the sea to his home in Leith on 21 October of this year, he set about beating his wife to death over a period of four days. The first cries were heard to come from the house at around 10 p.m. Between then and the 26th, beatings were both seen and heard to continue, before the woman was admitted to hospital, where she died on 5 November. Various neighbours both heard and saw the beatings but did nothing to prevent what was going on. On the 25th, Cumming locked his wife out of the house, and she attended a police station in order to get their help in gaining admittance. Despite her explaining to the police the cause of her many injuries, they did nothing but escort her home and make sure she was able to get back inside. It wasn't until Dr Brown of Leith Hospital was called to attend her on the 26th, and discovered her insensible and, in his opinion, suffering from brain damage caused by repeated blows to the head, that she was rescued from the situation, and the next day her husband arrested and charged with assault and, eventually, murder. Sentenced to death, he was hanged in January the following year.

23 OCTOBER 1790

The body of David Aikman, a young married man with six children, was discovered on this morning crushed in the mill wheel of the Canonmills. It was assumed that he had mistaken his path while passing the mill on the previous night, possibly under the influence of strong drink, and had fallen into the water just before the second wheel, which had then taken him up and broken his body in what the *Edinburgh Evening Courant* described as 'a manner too shocking for description.'

24 OCTOBER 1514

On this day there is a record of a trial of one Alexander Livingstone, 'indytit and accusit for the art and pairt of the creuall slauchter of umquhile Jak, upon the Borrowmuir of Edinburgh.'

This is the oldest existing record of a trial in Edinburgh. Livingstone was acquitted on the grounds of self-defence.

25 OCTOBER 1829

On the afternoon of this date, a Sunday, Mrs Catherine Franks and her daughter Madeline were seen at church in Haddington, East Lothian, and afterwards returned to their home in the outlying hamlet of Abbey. They were not seen alive again. Mrs Franks was a widow, whose husband had been a butler, and for whose service she received a pension from the Earl of Wemyss. She had a second daughter, who was away visiting an aunt in North Berwick. On the following Wednesday, a young man named James Storrie, believing the woman to have gone away and hearing the pig that she kept in the garden squealing in want of food, climbed the 6ft garden wall and found Mrs Franks mutilated body lying in the pigsty. She had received several blows to the head, and her throat had been cut. Raising the alarm, the house was entered and inside the body of Madeline, her skull battered in, was found lying under a carpet on the floor of the bedroom. It was assumed that the murder had been committed at some time on the Sunday evening. Mrs Franks' brother-in-law, Robert Emond, arrived from North Berwick to arrange the funeral and quickly became a suspect because of his manner. A check with the local authorities showed that he had been away from home on the night of the murder, and a search of his home showed that the clothes he had been wearing that day had been recently washed and that his boots matched with footprints found at the scene. It transpired that he had been accused by Mrs Franks of breaking open a box in her home containing money, and that he had had an argument with his wife on the Sunday afternoon, probably about the money in question, and she had locked him out of the bedroom. In his rage he had presumably struck out at the person he believed to be responsible for his troubles.

Broadsheet on the Haddington murders. (Author's Collection)

26 OCTOBER 1939

Tempted by the charms of an older woman, John Henry Connell, a man in his twenties who arrived in Edinburgh on 14 September of this year from his home in Dumfries, had a number of drinks on this night in the Grassmarket with 52-year-old Isabella Ralph, before she suggested that the pair retire to The Meadows to continue their liaison. However, along the way Connell found that £3 10s he had had on him was missing, and he accused the woman of stealing it. When she denied this, he struck her, and in the ensuing struggle he retrieved his money. However, when the woman began to scream he took her by the throat to quieten her, at which point she collapsed and, thinking she had fainted, Connell departed. The woman, however, was dead, her throat having been compressed by the force with which Connell had grasped her. She also had several broken ribs. Agreeing to plead guilty to the lesser charge of culpable homicide rather than murder, he was sentenced on this date to three years penal servitude.

27 OCTOBER 1930

At about eight o'clock on this morning, the lavatory attendant at Waverley railway station discovered the body of a man in one of the toilet cubicles on the north side of the station. The man had a bullet wound in his temple, and a revolver lying next to him suggested that he had taken his own life, although nobody on the station reported having heard a gunshot. Although a full description of the man and his possessions was printed in the newspapers, he appears to have remained unidentified.

28 OCTOBER 1551

Running feuds between clans were a frequent problem throughout Scotland in the Middle Ages. In this month the feud between the border clans of Scott and Kerr resulted in running battles on the streets of the capital, with Sir Walter Scott of Branxholm, the Laird of Buccleugh, losing his life in a brawl. An old ballad captures the tale:

Bards long shall tell
How Lord Walter fell!
When startled burghers fled afar,
The furies of the Border war,
When the streets of High Dunedin
Saw lances gleam and falchions redden,
And heard the slogan's deadly yell –
Then the chief of Branxholm fell!

29 OCTOBER 1935

Malcolm Sinclair Johnston, a medical supplies dealer, and a woman named Jane Ann Wo⌐ of Halifax, pleaded guilty on this date to having performed five illegal operations on w⌐ between 17 and 25 July of the same year, using an instrument obtained by Jo⊦ Of course, the operations referred to were backstreet abortions, and two of the fi⌐ later died as a result of the botched procedures. Johnston's wife, Sarah, was aˈ but charges against her were eventually dropped. The pair were both sentenc⌐ imprisonment.

BURKE'S HOUSE FROM THE BACK COURT.

A . Burke's Window .

B . Back entrance, where the Bodies were brought out .

William Burke's house where the murder of Mary Docherty took place. The window to Burke's room is marked with an 'A'. (Mary Evans Picture Library)

30 OCTOBER 1567

Bessie Tailefeir of Canongate, being convicted of slander, was sentenced on this day to be 'brankit, and set upon the cross for one hour.' The branks was a device also referred to as a 'scold's bridle'. It consisted of a metal frame which fitted around the head, with a sharp spike protruding into the mouth which made it impossible for the wearer to speak without spearing their tongue.

31 OCTOBER 1828: The West Port Murders

Burke and Hare's final victim was an Irishwoman named Mary Docherty, whom Burke met in a local tavern and enticed back to his home with a tale that his own mother was from the same town and that they might be related. This was the first time that a potential victim had been taken back to the Burkes' new lodgings, and a young couple, James and Ann Gray, who were lodging in the house at the time, met the lady. When she had disappeared the following morning, Ann Gray became suspicious; particularly when she was prevented by Burke from searching for her child's missing stockings in a pile of straw near the bed. Her curiosity getting the better of her, she returned later and found Docherty's body hidden in the straw. Running to fetch the police with her husband, the couple ran into Burke's common-law wife, Helen, who attempted to bribe them into silence, but they were unwilling to play along. Within the day both Burke and Hare, and their respective wives, were in prison and awaiting trial.

4

NOVEMBER

Greyfriars Kirkyard at night. (Lesley Gracie)

Queensberry House. (Alison Lang)

1 NOVEMBER 1942

On this date a patient at the Royal Infirmary in Edinburgh, who had been thought to be suffering from chickenpox, was diagnosed as actually a victim of smallpox. This began the first major smallpox epidemic in Scotland for over forty years. In total thirty-six people contracted the disease, and eight died, including a 12-year-old boy who was the second diagnosed victim, and thus the case that suggested that the disease was not an isolated incident. On 8 November the authorities ordered a mass vaccination campaign, and twenty-two vaccination centres were set up throughout the city. Ironically, there were ten deaths from Encephalitis, a common complication of the vaccination; more than died from the disease itself.

2 NOVEMBER 1697

This is the birth date of James Douglas, 3rd Marquess of Queensberry and formerly Earl of Drumlanrig. Douglas was quite insane and was kept locked up in Queensberry House in Edinburgh throughout his short life. In 1707, at the age of 10, on the day the Act of Union was signed, he escaped from his captivity as a result of the disturbances in the city that day. Feeling hungry he made his way to the kitchens, where he found a roaring fire and a scullery boy attending it. He quickly killed the boy, mounted his body on a spit and roasted it over the fire. He was found later having consumed a large portion of the flesh. He died in 1715 at the age of 17.

3 NOVEMBER 1709

Helen Bell was the servant of one John Strachan, a rich man who owned both the country mansion of Craigcrook in Corstorphine and a large house on the High Street in Edinburgh.

Bell was the keeper of the townhouse and, being left alone quite often, used it to meet with young gentlemen on a regular basis. On Halloween night of this year she entertained two men named William Thomson and John Robertson, to whom she happened to mention that the following Monday she would be going out to Craigcrook, thus leaving the house empty. On that Monday morning, as she locked up the house and began her journey, the two men appeared and told her they would accompany her part of the way. As they reached the foot of the Castle Rock, the men threw her down and bludgeoned her with a hammer, taking the keys and returning to rob the house, from which they stole a sum of money said to total £1,000. On the way, according to their confession, they swore that they would give their souls to the devil if one informed against the other. At this moment, they said, a stranger approached and offered to write them a bond to this effect, which they would then subscribe to in their own blood, an offer which they refused. The suggestion given was that the stranger was the devil himself.

4 NOVEMBER 1611

A curfew law was passed in Edinburgh on account of the 'night-walkers', persons who committed mischief under cover of darkness. Reference was made to those who 'commit sundry enormities upon his majesty's peaceable and guid subjects, not sparing the ordinar officers of the burgh, who are appointit to watch the streets of the same – of whom lately some has been cruelly and unmercifully slain, and others left for deid.'

5 NOVEMBER 1907

A verdict of 'not proven' was returned at the Sheriff's Court against James Denham and Thomas Barnes on a charge of having attacked two policemen with swordsticks and causing serious injury to both. Before giving his verdict, the Sheriff had spoken to criticise police methods in dealing with the matter. The two men had been seen by one of the officers, Alexander Lillie, a plain-clothes constable on vice duty, approaching a known prostitute on the corner of Rose Street. The men had accompanied her to Inverleith Park, shadowed by Lillie and another policeman, and when Barnes and the girl had lain down on a waterproof coat, the pair approached to effect an arrest. However, being in plain clothes, the pair assumed the two PCs to be robbers or scoundrels of some kind and set about defending themselves, only stopping when the girl assured them that they were policemen and known to her. The men pointed out in court that no impropriety had occurred, that their location had been in the open and not at all concealed, and that the girl in question was well known to them, and argued that they had been meeting socially and not in any 'professional' manner.

6 NOVEMBER 1828: The West Port Murders

The *Edinburgh Evening Courant* became the first newspaper to publish a report on the arrest of Burke and Hare on this date. On seeing a copy of this particular edition a short time later, Janet Brown, still concerned over the disappearance of her friend, Mary Paterson, realised the awful truth of what must have happened and went to the police with her story. However, the law were in a quandary, for although the miscreants' stories did not match, all were perfectly adamant that Mary Docherty had died of natural causes. If the Crown could not prove murder, there was no case, and in the case of Mary Paterson they did not even have a body to inspect. A third victim was soon added to the list of charges when a local shopkeeper recognised a pair of trousers that he had given to 'Daft Jamie' being worn by one of Constantine Burke's sons.

7 NOVEMBER 1730

The body of Baillie Glassford of Paisley was discovered at the foot of some cellar steps in the Canongate on this morning. He had been murdered and robbed of all his money on the previous night. A cook by the name of Alexander Punton was quickly apprehended and charged with the murder, one of the banknotes belonging to the man having been found in his possession. A further quantity of money was found in his house, despite the fact that he was known to be in debt. His wife claimed that he had found the money in the street. Another man named Cady, an associate of Punton, was also arrested after it was found that he had been inquiring in an alehouse after the Baillie on the night of the murder. It was also said that, following the old Scottish superstition, when Punton was asked to touch the body of the deceased man, it bled.

8 NOVEMBER 1856

Mary Wood was convicted on this day of killing her 11-day-old daughter by wrapping her in cloth and a towel together with a rock of 3lb or 4lb in weight and throwing her into the Union Canal. Wood was an unmarried woman who worked in a paper mill in Colinton, and had feared that she would lose her job through having a child out of wedlock. Initially, she told the authorities that she had left the child with its father, George McDonald, a baker at 112 Lawnmarket, but when they tried to locate him they found that no such man or address existed. She was sentenced to death, but later reprieved.

9 NOVEMBER 1928

Thirty-four-year-old Mary Mills was a pretty, single woman who worked in a picture framer's workshop in Rose Street, when she caught the eye of fellow employee James Marr. A married man, but separated from his wife, Marr began to make advances on Mary, who made clear her lack of interest. But Marr was not a man to take no for an answer and began to stalk Mary, often following her home at night and making lewd suggestions towards her. Her brothers and sisters began meeting her from work to protect her, and on 8 November, after an incident when Marr had showed her a knife and threatened to kill her, her sister Catherine persuaded her to complain to the police. That night Marr received an official visit from a policeman at his lodging house to warn him about his behaviour, but he was not home at the time. Informed of the visit by his landlady, he complained that his life had been ruined. When Robert Campbell, the foreman at the workshop, arrived the following morning at ten past eight, he found Mary lying dead on the floor, stabbed several times, and Marr with a self-inflicted throat wound, with blood also pouring from wounds to his wrists. On the table he had left a note confessing that he had done the deed because he loved her. Marr was taken to hospital where he recovered from his wounds. Found guilty of culpable homicide, he was sentenced to twelve years penal servitude.

10 NOVEMBER 1906

At about twenty past seven on this evening, David Anderson, the occupant of a flat in Graham Street, Leith, was just leaving the building when he saw something land with a crash on the pavement in front of him, and realised it was an unclothed newborn baby. Anderson took the child into the home of a neighbour where it survived until around one o'clock the following morning, when the doctors found that death was the result of a fractured skull. Matters had begun a year earlier when William Mitchell, a widower with five children aged between

12 and 3 who lived in the flat below Anderson, had advertised for a live-in housekeeper to look after his wards. Augusta Annie Grant, aged 20 at the time, applied for the job, and within a short time the pair had become intimate. However, when Annie fell pregnant, Mitchell tried to keep the fact a secret, ordering her not to go outside the house where people might see her condition. On the night of the birth, Mitchell had been in and out of the house to buy provisions, and also plainly stopped at a bar or two along the way – as he was said by witnesses to be clearly inebriated. He arrived back about five minutes after the child was born, Annie having taken it into bed with herself. Looking at the situation, he said 'this will not do', gathered up the child and departed. Mitchell was found guilty of culpable homicide.

11 NOVEMBER 1861

At midnight on the 10th, just as the bells of the city began to chime the new day, a tenement building at 107 High Street collapsed to the ground, having stood on the spot for 250 years. The building at the head of Baillie Fyfe's Wynd, though crumbling in some parts, had given no indication of being unsafe, and no warning was given to those within. During the early hours of the morning thirty-five bodies were pulled from the wreckage, along with a number of survivors, among whom was a young boy named Joseph McIvor who has gone down in Edinburgh history for his encouraging words to his rescuers, 'Heave awa' lads, I'm no deid yet!' The words were inscribed into the stonework of the building later erected on the spot, where they remain to this day. The building is known locally as the 'Heave Awa' Hoose'.

12 NOVEMBER 1636

Persons of the gypsy class having been proclaimed for some decades, a group of gypsies had been apprehended a month previously and had been held in prison at the village of Haddington in East Lothian since. However, the expense of keeping them having fallen on the people of the hamlet, the Sheriff applied to the Privy Council who decreed that all of the men and childless women should be put to death, the men by hanging and the women by drowning. Meanwhile, that 'such of the women as has children should be scourged through the burgh and burned on the cheek.'

Decoration on the 'Heave Awa' Hoose'. (Author's Collection)

13 NOVEMBER 1806

At five o'clock on this evening, William Begbie, a porter working for the British Linen Banking House, was found bleeding to death from a stab wound at the entrance to a passage leading to that institution's offices in Tweedale Court. He had been carrying £4,392 in large denomination notes from the bank's offices in Leith, and the money was now found to be missing. Despite a lengthy investigation, a reward of £500 offered, and several notorious persons of the city being taken for questioning, no information was found leading to any clue of the identity of the perpetrator. The only thing known was that Begbie was seen while passing up Leith Walk, apparently in the company of, or being dogged by, an unidentified man of stout appearance. The following year around £3,000 of the money was retrieved by some masons who found it rolled up and stuffed into a wall in the grounds of Bellevue House. Many years later suspicion for the killing fell on a deceased villain by the name of James Mackoull, who had been living very close to Tweedale Court at the time. A man fitting Mackoull's description was identified by a young seaman as the man following Begbie in Leith Walk, but he had not come forward at the time as he was engaged in a smuggling business when he made the observation. Furthermore, a Bow Street Runner by the name of Denovan claimed to have tackled Mackoull on the topic while he was in prison and received a violent response. Although all evidence is circumstantial, it seems likely that Mackoull was indeed the perpetrator of the crime.

14 NOVEMBER 1831

Thomas Beveridge stood trial on this date for the murder of his wife, Janet, at their home in the Canongate. A quarrel had arisen between them after he returned home from work to find his wife drunk in bed and his dinner not ready. The events were not witnessed, but neighbours heard a great commotion, and after Beveridge left the house, John Grant, a neighbour, entered and found Mrs Beveridge in such a dreadful state that he said she hardly looked like a human being. She died within a few hours, and a post-mortem examination showed she had been severely beaten with a fire poker and stabbed about the head with a blunt knife. Beveridge was sentenced to death and executed on 2 December.

15 NOVEMBER 1824

Among several fires that burned portions of Edinburgh, the fire that broke out on this date became known as the 'Great Fire'. It started in the premises of a copperplate printing house, within a seven-storey building which was soon entirely ablaze. Reaching the roof, it crossed to several adjoining tenements. Spreading swiftly, it moved to the timber buildings in the Cowgate, which burned up quickly, and it took until the middle of the following day before it was brought under control. No sooner had this first blaze ended than a second, probably ignited by a spark, began in the steeple of the Tron Kirk, which shortly thereafter collapsed. Meanwhile that same evening a third outbreak began in an eleven-storey building in Parliament Square and spread to parts of the court buildings. In all, ten people were killed over the course of two days and between 400 and 500 families were made homeless. The cost of the damage was estimated at £200,000, a considerable sum at that time.

16 NOVEMBER 1856

The arrest took place on this morning of Peter McLean, his wife Christina and a man named William Mansfield for the murder of one Thomas Maxwell on the road between Bathgate

The entrance to Tweedale Court, scene of the murder of William Begbie. (Author's Collection)

James Mackoull, probable murderer of William Begbie. (Author's Collection)

Ruins of the buildings in Parliament Square after the Great Fire. (Author's Collection)

and Durhamtown in West Lothian. The murder had occurred sometime around midnight on the previous night after Maxwell, together with his brother John, had left a public house in Bathgate to return to their home. The McLeans and Mansfield had been seen loitering on the road and threatening to 'do for' some people they were waiting for. According to John Maxwell, McLean ran towards him brandishing a knife and threatening to rip him, and as he dodged the blade Mansfield struck him with some heavy object and knocked him insensible. Shortly after this Neil McMullen and James Pollan intervened and chased the assailants away, although McLean was heard to say he would not leave until he had done for John Maxwell. McMullen detained him shortly, but released him after he said he would kill him too if he did not let him go. The reason for the argument between the men never came to light. McLean was sentenced to death and executed on 2 February the following year. Mansfield was found guilty of assault and sentenced to two years hard labour, and the case against McLean's wife was adjudged 'not proven'.

17 NOVEMBER 1897

A curious story appeared in the *Scotsman* on this date. It seemed that some three weeks previously a Russian woman by the name of Teresa Ulfeld, residing in a hotel in Leith Street, had reported to the police the loss of a purse containing between £10 and £20. Having no information to go on, little progress was made in the case, but three weeks later the woman returned and repeated that the purse had been stolen and asked for help to telegraph to friends in Russia for more money. Having little grasp of English, an interpreter was called and the woman was interviewed in a room in the central police office. After the interview the interpreter and the investigating officer had just stepped out to compare notes when a gunshot was heard from inside. Rushing back into the room they found that the woman had removed a revolver from her pocket and shot herself in the right temple. Quickly removed to hospital, she died within ten minutes of being admitted. It transpired that she had been acting strangely and threatening suicide for some days, after telling the story of the recent death of a lover, and a photograph of a handsome young man found among her possessions seemed to bear out this story.

18 NOVEMBER 1940

Jessie Sutherland, one of a pair of elderly sisters living together in Montgomery Street, was remanded in custody on a charge of attempted murder after younger sister Jane had been admitted to the Royal Infirmary on the previous Saturday night suffering from an axe wound to the head.

19 NOVEMBER 1825

A report in the *Scotsman* newspaper of this date describes a theft 'of a most base and unfeeling description.' A woman was sentenced in the Police Court for having deceived a young boy aged about 6 who had been employed by a gentleman to fetch for him a book in two volumes from a circulating library in the Horse Wynd. On his way back with the books, the woman persuaded the boy into a stair foot, where she stripped him naked and absconded with his clothes, the books and 5*d* in money that he carried on him. The woman was apprehended after offering the books to a stationer who recognised the library mark. She was sentenced to sixty days hard labour in the Bridewell Prison.

20 NOVEMBER 1699

Were the matter in hand not so serious, the malapropisms of convicted witch Margaret Myles on the day of her execution in Edinburgh might have been the stuff of a comedy sketch. Being asked to pray for her soul, she replied that she could not, as she had made a covenant with the devil and had renounced her baptism. Pressing on, the minister asked her to say the Lord's Prayer with him. However, when he spoke the line, 'Our father, who art in heaven,' she repeated with, 'Our father, who wert in heaven,' and would not say otherwise. When asked to say that she renounced the devil, she replied that she ounced him, and when told to state that she adhered to her baptism, she said instead that she hered it. Only at the very last, as she prepared for the final drop, did she say, 'Lord, take me out of the Devil's hands, and put me in God's.'

Facsimilile of part of William Burke's handwritten statement. (Mary Evans Picture Library)

21 NOVEMBER 1828: The West Port Murders

With Burke and Hare safely under lock and key, and with three murders now charged to their names, the state found it still had a serious problem. With only one body, and that showing no definite signs of foul play, they needed actual witness testimony to prove that murder had occurred. Unfortunately, the only possible witnesses were the criminals themselves, or their wives. It was decided that they would need to get one of the four to testify against the others. William Hare was finally settled upon, and at some point in late November he was offered immunity from prosecution if he agreed to tell his tale in court. In doing so, he also spared Maggie, as by law a person could not be forced to testify against their own spouse. As such it would be William Burke and Helen McDougal who would stand trial for the 'crimes of the century', while their counterparts, Hare and his wife, would walk free.

22 NOVEMBER 1728

A report in the *Edinburgh Evening Courant* tells of the chambermaid to a person of quality who, when objects were noticed missing from within the household, made accusation against several of the other servants for the theft of her master's goods. However, when a search of the house was made, the items in question were found within her own chests and she was accused of the theft. Whereupon, becoming quite unhinged as a result of this discovery, she was found to have hanged herself with her own apron strings.

23 NOVEMBER 1783

Under sentence of death for highway robbery, 18-year-old James Hay escaped on this day from the Tollbooth Gaol with the aid of his father, who, after partaking of liquor with one of the guards, persuaded him to run out and buy another bottle for them while, the door unguarded, young James slipped away into the night. Making his way down Beith's Wynd, he arrived at Greyfriars Kirk where, scaling the walls of the kirkyard, he broke into the gloomy mausoleum of 'Bluidy Mackenzie' and remained there among the bones of the dead for six weeks, hiding out from the authorities while being aided with food and supplies by former school friends from the nearby Heriot's Hospital.

24 NOVEMBER 1440

One of the more infamous events in Scottish history occurred at Edinburgh Castle on this date, an event that would come to be known as the Black Dinner. It occurred during the reign of King James II, who had come to the throne as a child and was yet only 10 years old. As the favourite councillor of his father, Sir Alexander Livingston of Callendar had become his guardian, and had made a deal with Sir William Crichton, the governor of the castle to make an attempt to control the throne through their influence on the boy King. James' mother, who shared the regency with the Earl of Douglas, had married Sir James Stewart, one of the supporters of the Douglas family. Convinced that the Douglases intended to seize control of the whole country, the pair set about a plan to crush this powerful family. Crichton convinced the young Earl that he should come to the castle to pay his respects to the King. Arriving in the company of his brother David and Sir Malcolm Fleming of Cumbernauld, according to the legend the three were greeted with great ceremony and treated to a banquet in the great hall. At the end of the banquet, a black bull's head was produced on the table; this being a Scottish custom indicating that the principle guests at a dinner would soon be dead. Immediately the three were seized and, in spite of the pleadings of James who begged for the lives of his new friends, they were swiftly beheaded in front of his eyes.

25 NOVEMBER 1945

This being a Sunday, four boys in their early teens from the Sighthill area of Edinburgh decided to take a walk in the Pentland Hills. Leaving their home in the morning they made their way out of the city and were near the village of Milton Bridge in the grounds of Kirkton Farm at around half past three that afternoon when they discovered an unexploded mortar shell. While examining their find the bomb detonated, and by the time Walter Stark, keeper of the nearby Glencorse Reservoir, reached the spot he found two of the boys, William McGuire and Edward Wilkinson, dead and the other two seriously injured. One of the pair, John Allen, died on the way to the Royal Infirmary.

26 NOVEMBER 1905

W.J. Watson, who had set himself up as a missionary in the city, was arrested on this date on a charge of bigamy. Watson, whose real name was Beck, had been married the previous year in Glasgow to a woman named Annie Allan. Her father, however, disapproved of the match and had taken his daughter home, whereupon Beck travelled to Edinburgh, changed his name, and started a 'City Slum and Rescue Mission', which was not officially affiliated to any legal or charitable body. Gathering a number of good souls around himself for the work, he romanced and married one of their number, Georgina Whytock, in August. However, Ms Allan had meantime broken away from her father's care and come to the city in search of her husband, whereupon his duplicity came to light. The mission itself was also somewhat suspect and had been criticised several times for possible false accounting, leading Watson to threaten legal action for libel.

27 NOVEMBER 1687

The superstition in medieval Scotland was that if the corpse of a murdered man was touched by his killer, the body would immediately pour forth an effusion of blood. When Sir James Stanfield was found drowned near his estate in Newmills, East Lothian, it was at first put down to suicide, but the haste with which his body was buried caused confusion, and a few days later some doctors were despatched from Edinburgh to exhume his remains and check for signs of foul play. The examination convinced them that death had been caused by strangulation. After their work was finished they turned the body back over to the family, but as his son Philip lifted the corpse to place it inside its coffin, blood was said to have poured out covering both his hands. Being instantly taken as a sign of his guilt, he was arrested and sent for trial. It transpired that he had been recently disinherited by his father on account of profligacy, and torture of the household servants provided ample other evidence of his evil. Philip Stanfield was executed on 24 February the following year, and during his hanging the rope slipped, causing him to fall onto his knees and the hangman to have to finish the job by strangulation. His body was then hung in chains on the Leith Road, from where it was twice stolen, the first time being found lying in a ditch in water. Together with the strangulation, this was taken as a sign that God had taken retribution for his crime.

28 NOVEMBER 1803

John Cowie was tried at the High Court of Justiciary on this date for the murder of his wife at their home in Borthwick's Close. Cowie was said to be a violent man who beat his wife Isobel often. For her part, she appears to have taken occasional forays into prostitution to pay for drink. On the night of 21 May, Cowie had returned from a trip to Glasgow to find his wife

Surgeon's Square. (Author's Collection)

drunk and insensible on the floor and had begun to beat her with a stick. When neighbours wrested the stick from him, he began instead to kick at his wife and jump up and down on her body, threatening to knock down any person who should interfere. After the beating, some of the neighbours helped the woman into bed; although all professed to know at that point that she would not survive. She expired at around three in the morning. Cowie was hanged for the crime on 4 January the following year.

29 NOVEMBER 1827: The West Port Murders

The Burke and Hare story began on this date when one of Hare's lodgers, a man named Donald, died. The man owed £4 in back rent, and together with Burke, Hare came up with a plan to retrieve his money. Removing the man from his coffin and replacing him with an equal weight in tree bark, they took the corpse to Surgeon's Square where they tried to locate the famous anatomist Dr Alexander Monro. Asking a student for directions, they were directed them to the rooms of Dr Robert Knox, who ran a private anatomy school in the square. Knox paid them £7 for the body, and on this night the germ of their plan was born that would result in one of the most notorious murder sprees in history.

30 NOVEMBER 1944

When summing up the case of murder against Stanley Braithwaite, accused of the murder of his wife who died after being stabbed eleven times in the body, arms and hands at their home in Bonnyrigg, the Lord Justice-Clerk stated that it was not enough, in cases such as these, for the purpose of the defence of diminished responsibility merely to show that an accused person had a very short temper, or was unusually excitable and lacking in self-control. The world, he pointed out, would be a very convenient place for criminals and a dangerous place for everyone else if that were the law. The defence had argued that Braithwaite, who had had a tempestuous childhood and had been wounded during the war, had a 'psychopathic constitution', and so, while not insane, was still only partially responsible for the attack on his wife. The jury, it seemed, disagreed and found him guilty. He was sentenced to death, this being later commuted to a life sentence.

DECEMBER

A gruesome grave marker in Greyfriars Kirkyard. (Author's Collection)

1 DECEMBER 1608

The barbarity involved in the burning of women unfortunate enough to be accused of witchcraft can seldom have been reported with such clarity than in an entry recorded in the minutes of the Privy Council for this date: 'The Earl of Mar declared to the Council that some women were taken in Broughton as witches, and being put to an Assize and convicted, albeit they persevered in their denial to the end, yet they were burned quick [alive] after such a cruel manner than some of them died in despair, renouncing and blaspheming; and others, half burned, brak out of the fire, but were cast quick in it again, till they were burned to the death.'

2 DECEMBER 1584

Another fire which threatened to engulf the town was started on this day by a young baxter's boy named Robert Henderson who, following some argument with his father, took his revenge by setting fire to a heather stack belonging to the parent which stood near to their house on the High Street, opposite the Tron. Starting the fire with gunpowder and a candle, it quickly went out of control and consumed the house, and was brought under control only with great difficulty before it began to spread. Henderson attempted to flee the town, but was apprehended and burned alive at the Mercat Cross as an example to others.

3 DECEMBER 1707

A salesman by the name of Guine in the service of an Africa company had obtained some services from a shoemaker in the Potterow named Hunter, and had paid him by leaving a factor for around £11 in wages, which had now come to be payable from the Equivalent, the sum of money granted to Scotland on the signing of the Act of Union. But when Hunter attempted to retrieve his money he found that certain of the signatures required were not possible to obtain, the persons involved being then away in London and not expected to return for a considerable time. Needing to obtain the cash, Hunter therefore became involved in a scheme with a pair of less-than-honest notaries to forge the signatures and draw the money. However, detection swiftly followed and Hunter and one of the notaries were tried and sentenced to be executed for their deception. They were hanged on 18 February the following year. The other notary and others involved in the scheme were spared only on the condition of voluntary banishment for life.

4 DECEMBER 1827

Andrew Ewart and Henry Pennycook were among a group of men who had agreed to stand watch over the graveyard at Libberton on this night to prevent bodysnatchers from violating the tombs of the recently deceased. After apprehending a group of 'resurrection men', Pennycook slipped away from the group unnoticed, believing he might have spotted an accomplice. Shortly afterwards Ewart did likewise and, seeing a shadowy figure moving among the graves, took up his firearm, loaded with swan shot, and fired at the man. Unfortunately it turned out to be Pennycook who, shot through the arm, died a few days later after gangrene set in to the wound. Ewart was charged with murder, it being an offence to fire a gun without express permission of the magistrates, and was sentenced to death, although he was later reprieved.

*Libberton Church
and graveyard.
(Author's Collection)*

5 DECEMBER 1863

One of the serious dangers faced by miners in the Lothian coalfields was that of 'fire damp.' A natural gas, this occurs when porous rocks adjacent to a coal seam are placed under great pressure by an overlying bed of non-porous rock. The gas is composed chiefly of highly flammable methane. The *Scotsman* of this date reported on two accidents involving 'fire damp' in West Lothian collieries during the same week. In the first, a young 13-year-old miner named George Snadden, died and his father, Alexander, was severely injured when a 'fire damp' explosion occurred as the younger man worked at the face with a mash hammer. In the other, two miners named Charles Brown and Alexander Robertson were severely burned when their lamps ignited the 'fire damp' as they examined a working which had been flooded.

6 DECEMBER 1858

Mary McGill and her sister Margaret had come from Inverness four years earlier to try their luck in the city, and while Margaret had fallen on good fortune and become respectably married, Mary, who was illiterate and partially deaf, had not been so lucky. Meeting a sailor from Leith named Thomas Stewart, she soon after fell pregnant. A marriage was swiftly arranged, but before it took place Stewart reneged and refused to go through with it. Unable to work because of her situation, and her sister being unwilling to help, Mary ended up in the workhouse. The child, a girl, was born at the end of November, and on 4 December Mary threw herself again on the mercy of her sister, living then in Gilmour Street, and was allowed to stay for a couple of days, but then it was decided that she must return to the workhouse. Margaret's neighbour, a Mrs Strachan, accompanied her to make arrangements, and then agreed that Mary could stay in her house for the night. On the way back, while

149

Edinburgh charity workhouse. (Author's Collection)

passing along Nicholson Street, Strachan noticed Mary fall behind her for a time near a chemist shop, but thought nothing of it. That night, when her husband returned home, the baby was lying on his bed and, wishing to get some rest, he asked Mary to remove it. When she picked it up she turned to him with the words, 'Archie, I think the bairn is dead.' It was quickly ascertained that such was the case, and that it had been dead for some time. On being questioned, and asked if she had given the baby anything, Mary replied that she had given it salt and water because it had seemed to have a bad stomach and she had wanted to make it vomit. But later she admitted that she had given it a powder used for cleaning bonnets, the main ingredient of which was oxalic acid, which she had purchased at the chemist in Nicholson Street. Claiming she had not meant to kill the child but just make it sick, when she realised what had happened Mary took some of the acid herself, but had her stomach pumped before it could have any effect on her.

7 DECEMBER 1597

An illustration of the unusual value placed on human life in medieval Edinburgh occurred on this day. Archibald Jardine, master stabler to the Earl of Angus, was killed accidentally or 'by some negligence' by a young man named Andrew Stalker at the head of Niddry's Wynd. Stalker was quickly apprehended and put in prison to await his fate, however, being a popular man in the town, his friends rallied round in an attempt to spare him. They went to Angus and offered to serve as an army for him at whatever time he might be in need if, in return, he would spare Stalker's life and have him released from the prison. As the slain man was his servant, and thus he was considered to be the wronged party, he was fully entitled to do so, and agreed readily to the terms, so that Stalker was granted his liberty on the same day.

8 DECEMBER 1949

An altercation over the price of a house led to murder on this date when Andrew Donaldson, a young man from Temple in Midlothian, went to the cottage of 76-year-old Charles Armstrong Turnbull, which he had been hoping to buy, in order to negotiate a fair deal with him. According to Donaldson's original story, the pair met at 6 o'clock on 7 December, when Donaldson gave the older man £90 towards the purchase of the cottage and arranged to meet him the next day to attend his solicitors in Edinburgh. The appointment, he said, was not kept by the other man. At 9.30 p.m. on the night of the 8th, Mr Turnbull's neighbour, a Mr John Amos, sensing something was wrong because of the whining of dogs inside the cottage, broke in and found Turnbull lying dead in the fireplace. He had been savagely beaten. Under questioning, Donaldson eventually admitted that he had done the deed, but said that it had been carried out in a blind rage after Turnbull attempted to squeeze more money out of him after a deal had already been struck. Despite his defence attempting to argue that Donaldson's own statements were contradictory and that he was not in his right mind when he made them, the court found him guilty of murder, and he was sentenced to death.

9 DECEMBER 1823

Fifteen-year-old John Reid was relieved on this day to receive a commutation of his death sentence on account of his youth. He had been convicted, along with Thomas Black, of breaking into the home of Alexander White in South Leith and making away with clothing and silver cutlery of high value. Despite Reid having been described as a thoroughly bad character, known to the police for over three years, and Black having been merely his willing accomplice, the other boy was not so lucky. Just a few months older than his friend, Black met his end at the gallows the following day. Before his execution he made a speech from the platform, calling on all children to observe the Sabbath day, and saying that it was not doing so that had led him into his wicked ways.

10 DECEMBER 1613

A large English warship which had been laid up at Leith Harbour for six weeks was almost ready to set sail once more when one of her crew, an Englishman, notwithstanding that his son was on board, laid trails of powder throughout the vessel and set it alight. Sixty men were on board at the time, although the captain and first mate were on shore stocking provisions for the journey. The ship was destroyed utterly, burned down to her keel, and twenty-four of those on board perished. Efforts to extinguish the blaze and rescue the men were hampered by the fact that the fire had set the ordinance on board to explode or to fire, forcing everyone to keep their distance.

11 DECEMBER 1953

When little Leslie Sinclair and her friend Margaret Johnston did not return home after going out to play on the afternoon of this date, their parents began to worry. By the time the evening drew in and darkness fell, their worry turned to something worse, and Margaret's father set off in search of the two children, neither one of whom was more than 5 years old. Learning that the children were not at any relative or neighbour's house, the police were swiftly called. Within the hour, search parties with torches spread out across the area from Leith Walk as far as Calton Hill, the area in which the two girls lived. Every street, building and hedgerow was searched diligently, but with no sign of the pair being found. Meanwhile, at 5 Marshall's

Greyfriars Kirk. (Author's Collection)

Court, the tenement building where Leslie lived, tenants who found themselves unable to get into the shared lavatory forced the door and finally made the discovery. The two girls were dead, savagely beaten around the head and the face. One of the tenants, John Lynch, a 45-year-old Irishman, had been well acquainted with the girls who called him 'Uncle Paddy'. He had involved himself with the search, and bought Lesley's mother a drink to calm her nerves while the whole affair was going on. When the police began to question the residents, he kept trying to interrupt them, and they believed him to be drunk. When they finally got round to entering his tenement flat they noticed that he had blood on his sleeve, and an apron string from the clothing of one of the girls was found lying in the room. Lynch was swiftly taken into custody and charged with sexual assault and murder. He was found guilty by a unanimous verdict, and hanged on 23 April of the following year.

12 DECEMBER 1696

The Church, still considered at this time the most suitable arbiters of what would best serve the people, declared a fast on this date to assuage the wrath of God which, the edict acknowledged, was 'very visible against the land, in the judgements of great sickness and mortality in most parts of the kingdom, as also of growing dearth and famine threatened, with the imminent hazard of ane invasion from our cruel and bloody enemies abroad; all the just deservings and effects of our continuing and abounding sins, and of our great security and impenitency under them.'

13 DECEMBER 1946

At about half past midnight, David Boggie, a middle-aged seaman, opened the door of his home at 20 Coatfield Lane, Leith, to find himself in a world of trouble. Outside were the three Rodgers brothers; Patrick, John and James, whose mother had been having an affair with

Boggie for the past twenty years. She had visited him earlier in the evening in the company of another woman, Mrs Easton, and on her return she ran into her sons while crossing Leith Links. When they asked where she had been, she answered truthfully, and they said that they would go and speak to the man. In his dying deposition, Boggie claimed that the men attacked him the moment they walked through the door, and that Patrick Rodgers had picked up a knife lying by the sink and stabbed him with it. The brothers, on the other hand, claimed that heated words had been exchanged between them when Boggie had taken up the knife and threatened them with it. In their struggle to disarm him they fell on him and the knife went into his body. Forensic evidence, such as there was, suggested that Boggie had, indeed, been holding the knife and been disarmed in some way. At trial the jury convicted Patrick of culpable homicide, and acquitted his two brothers.

14 DECEMBER 1753

Reported in the *Edinburgh Evening Courant*: 'William Mill, tailor in the Potterow, having missed his way as he was coming home through the Meadow, fell into one of the ditches, and was next morning taken up dead.'

15 DECEMBER 1941

While home on leave before being sent to a new posting, young soldier Peter McLaren was cleaning his battledress at his home at 9 St Stephen's Place when he failed to notice that some of the petrol he was using had spilled onto the mattress of the bed where his wife and 3-month-old child were sleeping. Later that morning, at around 8 a.m., McLaren returned to the room to find the mattress smouldering. When he tried to arouse his wife he found that she had asphyxiated in her sleep from the fumes. The child was still breathing, but died later in the day due to the lung damage sustained.

16 DECEMBER 1828

Reported in the *Scotsman*: 'A respectable elderly gentleman, while passing down the western side of North St Andrew's Street, where there are usually few passengers, was attacked by several ruffians, who knocked him down, and, after subjecting him to further maltreatment, robbed him of his watch. The injuries he received are of so serious a nature as to require surgical attendance.'

17 DECEMBER 1600

Equality of the sexes is something of a modern concept, and in medieval Scotland if a nobleman had ambitions on a particular unwed woman, abduction was a not uncommon method of obtaining his ends. Such was the case with John Kincaid of Craig House, on the slope of Craiglockhart Hill, when he aimed his desire at a young widow by the name of Isobel Hutcheon, then living in the village of Water of Leith. Kincaid, together with a party of friends and servants, rode to the village and, breaking down the door of the home of Baillie John Johnson where she was living, 'pat violent hands on the said Isobel's person, took her captive, reft, ravished, and took her away with him.' As it so happened, King James VI was riding nearby and heard of the abduction, and rode personally together with the Earl of Mar and others to Craig House to relieve the young lady. Kincaid was arrested and stood trial and, found guilty, was granted his liberty but fined 2,500 merks and his brown horse.

Water of Leith village. (Author's Collection)

18 DECEMBER 1884

John Fortune, a gamekeeper in the employ of the Earl of Rosebery on his estate just outside Edinburgh, died on this day in the home of his fellow gamekeeper, James Grosset. Fortune and Grosset, together with a third man, rabbit-trapper John McDiarmid, had been shot while attempting to apprehend a pair of poachers named Robert Vickers and William Innes. Coming across the men three days earlier, they had ordered them to stand. The pair raised their guns and fired, striking Fortune and Grosset first, and McDiarmid shortly after. Fortune instantly stated that he had been struck in the heart, but Grosset, who had only taken four balls of shot across his back, was able to move and ran for assistance to a nearby farm. On his death, Fortune was found to have fifty-two shot pellets in his body. McDiarmid, who lingered until 6 January before succumbing to his injuries, had thirty-eight. The two poachers were found guilty of murder, and executed in March of the following year.

19 DECEMBER 1791

A sensational appearance at the High Court of Justiciary on this date was one James Plunkett, who had been subject to an intense manhunt since his escape from the Glasgow Tollbooth on 26 October. Plunkett, a former soldier, had been convicted in Glasgow on a charge of robbery after convincing silversmith Robert Dundas to accompany him to a secluded spot and then threatening him with a cutlass. Sentenced to death, he broke out of the prison along with a number of other men, injuring his leg in the process, the scar from which was frequently reported as a distinguishing feature by which he could be recognised. He was eventually apprehended in Arbroath and brought to the capital for a hearing to decide if he should be returned to Glasgow to face his original punishment. This being agreed to be the case, he was executed on 11 January the following year.

20 DECEMBER 1862: The West Port Murders

Despite his illustrious career as an anatomist and surgeon, including many publications and appointments to prestigious institutions, including the London Cancer Hospital, Dr Robert Knox, who died on this date at the age of 71, would forever be best remembered for his involvement with Burke and Hare and the West Port murders. Knox was Edinburgh-born and bred, the eighth child of a teacher, he arrived in the world on 4 September 1791 and was educated at the Royal High School. In 1810 he began to study medicine, and after a stint at St Bartholomew's Hospital in London he enlisted in the Army and served as an assistant surgeon at a field hospital in Brussels, and later at the Cape of Good Hope. In 1821 he went to France to study anatomy, and a year later returned to his native Edinburgh where he was elected a fellow of the Royal Society. He was appointed Conservator of a museum of anatomy, which had been established at his own proposal, and started a private anatomy school in Surgeon's Square, the establishment to which the two West Port ruffians had brought the victims of their crimes. After the murders he attempted to continue his career as before, but found his reputation in tatters. In 1831 he was forced to resign his position at the museum, and by 1840, with few students willing to study under him, he closed his school. Moving to London, for the next sixteen years he earned his living mostly from medical journalism and lectures, until his appointment to the cancer hospital in 1856. His work there was exemplary and somewhat restored his reputation in the remaining six years of his life.

21 DECEMBER 1682

Just as is the case today, a last will and testament at this time was only considered valid if it was made while the testator was provably of sound mind. How this was achieved was that he should appear afterwards 'at kirk and market', allowing people to thus see him and testify to his state of health. Thomas Carmichael, however, had a plan to cheat the rightful heirs of Daniel Mure of Gledstanes out of their inheritance. Mure being on his deathbed, Carmichael induced him to make a disposition of his estate in his own favour. Then, with the aid of a writer by the name of William Chiesley, they dressed up Carmichael's servant Thomas Bell to impersonate the sick man, and to go about in this manner as well as attending a notary to have the new will approved. The notary in question was so unsure that the person before him was Mure that he made the man swear an oath on the Bible. When Mure died, his brother Francis, who had expected to inherit the estate that had been in their family for generations, became suspicious of the new will, and brought the matter before the Privy Council on this date. The whole affair was exposed, and Carmichael was punished by a fine of 5,000 merks, 2,000 of which were payable directly to Francis Mure, while Chiesley was also fined 3,000 merks.

22 DECMEBER 1923

A bizarre theory became the talking point after a murder and suicide tragedy in Rodney Street on this date. The landlady of the tenement building where Frederick Allen and his wife Clara had taken rooms was startled to hear shots ring out at about twenty minutes to two in the afternoon. Rushing to the room, the door was opened by Allen who was bleeding profusely from a wound in his head. 'For God's sake, fetch a policeman and a doctor, I am bleeding to death!' he shouted. The landlady saw Mrs Allen lying motionless on the floor and at once

Dr Robert Knox. (S.P. Evans)

ran for assistance, and as she reached the landing a third shot was heard. A policeman and an ambulance were summoned, but when they returned to the apartment both husband and wife were dead. However, a mystery soon surrounded the actual events in the room. Mr Allen had clearly shot his wife before turning the gun on himself, that much was certain. However, investigators soon found that the third shot fired from the gun had missed Mr Allen entirely and been fired straight into the ceiling, meaning that the bullet wound that the landlady had seen was the cause of death. However, the post-mortem examination showed that that wound had passed through the brain causing such damage as to have brought about death instantaneously. It was therefore hypothesised that when Mr Allen answered the door to his landlady he was, to all intents and purposes, already dead, and that his body was merely following the electrical impulses of the last thoughts that passed through his mind during life. The third shot had most likely been fired when all nerve activity finally ceased and Mr Allen's body fell to the floor.

23 DECEMBER 1696

Thomas Aikenhead has become something of a *cause célèbre* after being sentenced on this day to be executed for the crime of blasphemy. His indictment stated that: 'The prisoner has repeatedly maintained, in conversation, that theology was a rhapsody of ill-invented nonsense, patched up partly of the moral doctrines of philosophers, and partly of poetical fictions and extravagant chimeras. That he ridiculed the Holy Scriptures, calling the Old Testament 'Ezra's Fables' in profane allusion to *Easop's Fables*. That he railed on Christ, saying, he had learned magic in Egypt, which enabled him to perform those pranks, which were called miracles.

That he called the New Testament the history of the impostor Christ. That he said Moses was the better artist and the better politician, and he preferred Mohammed to Christ. That the Holy Scriptures were stuffed with such madness, nonsense, and contradictions, that he admired the stupidity of the world in being so long deluded by them. That he rejected the mystery of the Trinity as unworthy of refutation, and scoffed at the incarnation of Christ.' Aikenhead, a student at the University of Edinburgh, attempted to save his own life by repenting and recanting on his previous utterances, but all was in vain and the prosecution demanded the death penalty as a warning to others who might express such ideas in the future. Resigning himself to his death, the young man prepared a lengthy speech which he delivered on the gallows on the afternoon of 8 January 1697, in which he explained himself as a seeker after truth, and described morality as a human rather than a divine invention. He was the last person to be executed for this particular crime in any part of the British Isles.

24 DECEMBER 1828: The West Port Murders

The trial of William Burke and Helen McDougal for the West Port murders opened on the morning of Christmas Eve at the High Court of Justiciary in Edinburgh. Crowds lined the street to watch all the way as the murderer was transported from the Calton Gaol to Parliament Square. The courtroom itself was crowded with reporters, Members of the Faculty and Writers to the Signet, with no room left for members of the public to spectate. Burke was charged with the three murders, of Mary Paterson, James Wilson and Mary Docherty, while Helen was charged only with involvement in the last of the three offences. Defence council objected both to their being tried together and to their being tried on more than one offence. The first of these objections was thrown out, and the second answered by the compromise that the three offences would be heard separately, such that prosecution was instructed to proceed initially as if trying the case for the murder of Mrs Docherty only. The result of this ruling was that neither Dr Knox nor any of his assistants took the stand, as they had been called to testify to events of the earlier two murders. Knox's doorkeeper, David Paterson, did testify, but only as to events of the night of 31 October and its aftermath. The key witness, of course, was William Hare, who described the whole events of the night of the murder, albeit claiming that the killing itself was performed by Burke alone. He also described how the two women had run from the room the moment the murder began. Possibly as a result of this testimony, the case against Helen McDougal was found 'not proven', and she was dismissed. Burke was found guilty as charged, and sentenced to be executed on 28 January, and fed on nothing but bread and water in the interim.

25 DECEMBER 1680

For Christmas Day let us tell a rather less gruesome tale than some in this book. A man was burned on this day, but in effigy only, rather than in real life. The man in question was the Pope, and his assailants were a group of students from the University of Edinburgh who, knowing that the Duke of York, later to be King James VII, was then present in the city and was privately of the Catholic persuasion, intended this act as a protest and a warning against any attempt to revert the realm to that faith. The effigy itself was a wooden statue, although a portrait had also been prepared and sent to Castle Hill to act as a decoy. As the soldiery of the city were thus diverted, the effigy was marched up Blackfriars' Wynd to the High Street. The statue itself was hollow and filled with gunpowder, such that when the boys placed it down and set it alight it burned for a time, and then exploded sending pieces scattered across the street. The head was carried up to Castle Hill by a number of boys, while the rest were scattered by troops led by the Earl of Mar and Lord Linlithgow, who arrived in such great haste that he fell off his horse.

26 DECEMBER 1838

On receiving a verdict of Culpable Homicide against Joseph Hagan for the killing of his wife, Lord Cockburn stated that it was the most aggravated case of homicide he had ever known. According to the evidence, Hagan had returned home from transacting some business in Leith and, finding her in bed and believing her to be drunk, had dragged her to the kitchen where he began to beat her with a stick. He then proceeded to kick and trample on her, took a chair and placed it on her stomach and jumped on it several times, and finally took some broken glass and smashed it down on her. According to Mary Docherty, the deceased woman's 10-year-old niece who was present during the attack, the beating continued for more than twenty minutes. After the beating was over, he removed his wife's clothes and cleaned her and put her into her bed. Mrs Hagan was still alive the following morning, and spoke to the child saying that she wished her sister were there. Later that morning the sister, a Mrs More, arrived and was told by the girl that 'my uncle killed my aunt last night.' When she went through to see her sister she found that she was, indeed, dead. Denied by the verdict the opportunity to pass the death penalty, Hagan was sentenced to be transported for life.

27 DECEMBER 1843

Of the circumstances of the murder of John Geddes very little was known, and the apprehension and conviction of James Bryce was a feat of remarkable detective work for the time. Even the date of the murder was not certain, as Geddes' body was not discovered until five days after the incident when neighbours began to worry that he had not been seen or heard from. Bryce, who was a brother-in-law of the deceased, was traced through a watch he had stolen from the dead man and then pawned, and when apprehended he was also found to be in possession of the man's belt, and his son was in possession of his shoes which Bryce had given to him. He had also, in the days after the murder, spent a great deal of money despite having professed to be nearly broke before it. Furthermore, witness testimony showed that he left his home in Coatbridge, Lanarkshire that morning, and had walked east to such an extent that he could be placed within six miles of Geddes' home outside West Calder. Before his execution, Bryce produced a lengthy written confession in which he detailed the crime, claiming that he had gone to Geddes to get money for his daughter's wedding, but had lied and claimed it was for a child's funeral. Geddes had helped him with money previously, but on this occasion refused, and an argument broke out between the pair whereupon Bryce took up a pair of fire tongs and beat the man insensible before strangling him with a cord. Murder, it seems, ran in the family, as twenty years later his nephew George Bryce would also be executed for the murder of Jane Seton in Ratho.

28 DECEMBER 1822

The *Scotsman* newspaper of this date contains a report on the resurrection trade: 'Saturday morning, about six o'clock, two men and a gig were observed by some country people on the road from Dalkeith, and entertaining suspicion that they were conveying dead bodies to town, they followed them till they reached the Gibbet Toll, when they communicated their suspicions to the watchman on duty, who stopped the gig, and on examining it found the bodies of a woman and child, which had been disinterred early that morning from some burying-ground to the south of Dalkeith. One of the men made his escape; the other, with the gig and its contents, was conveyed to the police office. The bodies were in a large boot or basket in the back of the vehicle, similar to a dogcart, but of extraordinary dimensions. The man has been handed over to the Sheriff for prosecution.'

29 DECEMBER 1592

A feud between clans in the upper valley of the Tweed spilled over onto the streets of Edinburgh on this day when James Geddes, who had been in the city for some eight days, was set upon by members of the Tweedie family whose clan head, the Laird of Drummelzier, feared an attack on his person from the man. The Tweedies had built steadily a plan whereby they had placed spies in the house where Geddes lodged, and in other locations he was in the habit of visiting. On the day in question, Geddes was in the Cowgate getting his horse shod at the booth of David Lindsay when Drummelzier was informed of his whereabouts and decided the time was right for action. Dividing his men, he had one party move down Conn's Close, opposite the blacksmith's booth, while he and two other members of the Tweedie clan passed down Kirk O'Field Wynd, west of Geddes' position. On emerging from the Wynd they saw him standing at the booth door and, taking up pistols, shot him down in cold blood.

30 DECEMBER 1818

Executed by hanging on this day was Robert Johnston, who, in company with George Galloway and James Lees, assaulted and robbed a candlemaker by the name of John Charles in the early morning of 25 October. Charles had spent the previous evening in the company of three friends in a house in Fleshmarket Close, and left at around midnight. Heading home, he had just passed St Patrick Square when he was attacked by the three men. Crying out for assistance, one of the men pointed a pistol at him saying, 'Damn you, do you see that? If you call out again, I will blow your brains out.' The men then rolled him into a ditch, and while one held him by the throat, the others ransacked his clothes and stole money and bills amounting to over £600. The three were quickly apprehended based on Charles's descriptions, but had already lodged the money with a man named Munoch, a servant who, suspicious of its nature, asked his master for advice. The money was consequently given to a solicitor who recognised it as the proceeds of the robbery and immediately informed the police. Galloway and Lees pleaded guilty at trial, and were given terms of transportation, while Johnston pleaded not guilty, resulting in the death sentence being passed against him.

The head of Fleshmarket Close.
(Author's Collection)

31 DECEMBER 1811

A band of young men referred to as 'artisans and idlers' formed an organised mob to take advantage of the New Year celebrations on this night. They set forth through the streets with bludgeons and batons, striking down and robbing every person who came within their path. The City Watch were helpless to prevent the rioting, and the one watchman who did try to halt their progress was killed on the spot. The situation continued until two in the morning, mostly concentrated in the centre of the High Street near the heads of Stamp Office Close and Fleshmarket Close. Four of the young desperadoes were captured and tried for the crimes, and three were hanged on 22 April of the following year.

Other local titles published by The History Press

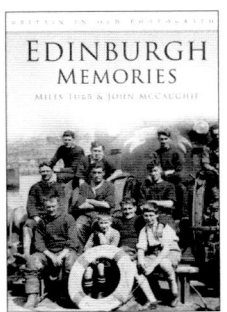

Edinburgh Memories
MILES TUBB & JOHN MCCAUGHIE

Edinburgh Memories is the unique and fascinating result of many conversations and interviews with local people, recalling life in their city between the two world wars. Vivid memories are recounted, including childhood and schooldays, work and play, sport and leisure. Anyone who knows Edinburgh will be amused and entertained, surprised and moved by these stories, which capture the unique spirit of Scotland's capital city.

978 0 7509 5100 5

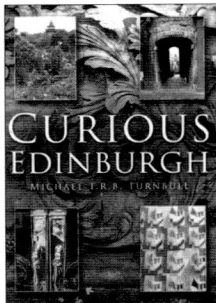

Curious Edinburgh
MICHAEL T.R.B. TURNBULL

A guide to more than 100 of the curious and interesting corners of Edinburgh, *Curious Edinburgh* explores the hidden treasures of Scotland's capital city and unlocks the forgotten meaning of landmarks that have become familiar. It tells the reader how to find and understand the city's nooks and crannies, and includes information on access to all the sites covered. The book is illustrated with more than 120 modern and historic photographs and line drawings.

978 0 7509 3949 2

Edinburgh Old Town
SUSAN VARGA

In this beautiful collection of 200 images from the Edinburgh Room, Susan Varga presents a pictorial history of Edinburgh's Old Town. The images include the Royal Mile, Castlehill, the Lawnmarket, High Street, Canongate, Grassmarket and the George IV Bridge, as well as the royal residences of Holyrood House and Edinburgh Castle. Many date from the early years of photography and give a unique perspective on the social conditions of the time.

978 0 7524 4083 5

Haunted Edinburgh
ALAN MURDIE

This chilling collection of tales contains never before published cases of hauntings, phantoms and poltergeists in the Edinburgh area. Revealing heart-stopping accounts of apparitions, manifestations and related supernatural phenomena, it takes the reader on a tour of the city's streets and buildings, through convents, cellars, churches and attics. Illustrated with more than 70 images, *Haunted Edinburgh* will delight everyone with an interest in the supernatural.

978 0 7524 4356 0

Visit our website and discover thousands of other History Press books. **www.thehistorypress.co.uk**